MMA

» LESSONS «

Every Technique You Need to Know about Fighting

Triumph Books
542 South Dearborn Street
Suite 750
Chicago, Illinois 60605
(312) 939-3330
Fax (312) 663-3557
www.triumphbooks.com

Printed in U.S.A.
ISBN: 978-1-60078-408-8

TABLE OF CONTENTS

TABLE OF CONTENTS

WRESTLING

65 – 114

TABLE OF CONTENTS

SUBMISSIONS

115 - 175

If you are reading this book, we already have something in common. I have no idea if you are a professional fighter who graces these pages showing techniques, a die-hard fan flipping through some of his favorite moves to watch, a martial arts beginner looking to improve his skills or even someone who has no idea what they are looking at but has a curiosity to remedy.

When we set out to create the be-all, end-all of mixed martial arts (MMA) techniques, we knew it would be a tough task. Even though we've collected hundreds of moves from the best fighters in the world over the years for our award-winning technique section for *TapouT Magazine*, the real challenge was deciding which techniques *wouldn't* make the cut.

Whether you enjoy the flashy striking styles of Anderson Silva, the fluid Brazilian jiu-jitsu of Rigan Machado or the bone-crushing wrestling of Greg Nelson, there is something in here for you. Organized in three categories (striking, wrestling and submissions), this book will serve as your guide through the unlimited techniques of the finest arts in the world that make up MMA.

That is all we can provide in one book, a guide. As the sport continues to grow and the fighters evolve, the game continues to take on a life of its own. As fighters the world over continue to develop new techniques and master the old, we do our best to keep up with the ever-changing world of MMA and bring that to you. Who knows? Maybe one day you will appear in the pages of our next book showing the world the art you have worked so hard to master.

If you are reading this book, you have been captivated in some way by mixed martial arts. And that is what we have in common.

RJ Clifford
Editor, Fighter, Fan

IN THE BEGINNING

In every part of the world exists some form of martial arts that has been passed down from generation to generation. Throughout time many of these arts have evolved from hand-to-hand combat to pure sport, from the battlefield to the ring. While there have been numerous martial artists who have stuck to the budo code, many were unwilling to shed their traditional trappings to evaluate the bigger picture of what worked and why. Television and film further perpetuated an almost mythical quality about martial arts that flooded dojos with would-be masters looking to hone these ancient skills.

Many believe mixed martial arts (MMA) is what the late Bruce Lee envisioned with his notes on martial arts, fighting, cross-training and physical fitness. Lee may have been the king of chop-socky onscreen, but his philosophy led to a real study of martial arts, which ultimately became the book, *Tao of Jeet Kune Do*. In this book one can find chapters on stand-up, grappling and submissions. The opening scene in *Enter the Dragon* features Lee utilizing all three to subdue a rotund opponent; it was a key scene that Lee scripted and directed himself.

Over 40 years later, the mystique of the martial arts has been replaced by this evolutionary combative sport where elite athletes combine striking, wrestling and submission holds in ways that continue to inspire. Fighters come from all walks of life to test their diverse backgrounds that have kept audiences, at home and in person, glued to the action in front of them. From spectacle to sport, MMA has changed the martial arts world forever, but where did it come from?

In the 33rd Ancient Greek Olympics in 648 B.C., *pankration* (meaning "all strength" or "all power") was introduced as a way to find the best athlete among wrestlers and boxers (known as pugilists). The rules were barbaric and the fights were rudimentary, but it's fair to say this was the first recorded form of MMA in history. Though pankration was eventually banned from the Olympics, the mixing of different fighting disciplines became commonplace all across the globe.

Japanese martial artist Jigoro Kano took the most effective techniques from jujutsu (which covered a wide range of arts, empty hand and weapons) to create judo. In 1898, he wrote, "By taking together all the good points I had learned of the various schools and adding thereto my own inventions and discoveries, I devised a new system for physical culture and moral training as well as for winning contests." Though Kano's original judo became watered down to primarily throwing techniques, it was one of his students, Mitsuyo "Conde Koma" Maeda, who would carry the torch. Maeda was a rogue judoka who traveled the world competing in contests for money, and one such trip took him to Brazil.

In 1917, 14-year-old Carlos Gracie watched one of Maeda's demonstrations, and with the aid of his father and prominent businessman, Gastão, he started taking judo lessons. Although there is some disagreement as to how and when the name changed from judo to jujutsu to Brazilian jiu-jitsu, there is no question that the Gracie family led a martial arts revolution with the grappling art. Focusing primarily on ground fighting and clean submission techniques over striking, brother Helio Gracie, and his huge extended family, defended the art by challenging anyone throughout the 1900's. Boxers, kickboxers, capoeira stylists and other worthy contenders didn't last long against the Gracie clan in matches that were dubbed by a Brazilian news reporter as *vale tudo* (meaning "anything goes").

Vale tudo matches became a big hit on Brazilian television, and even though Brazilian jiu-jitsu was no competition for soccer, it proved itself time and time again by taking all the tools away from the stand-up fighter and forcing him out of his element. When Helio's son, Rorion, came to the United States in 1978, he wanted to teach the art to anyone who would listen. Becoming an actor for a string of television shows, Rorion invited stars and directors to his garage for lessons, but Brazilian jiu-jitsu (or Gracie Jiu-Jitsu)

had a difficult time going up against the fancier moves of karate and kung fu. The grappling arts just weren't as "cool" as the high-flying kicks; even Rorion's work with Mel Gibson in the original *Lethal Weapon* hardly gave notice to the art.

ULTIMATE EVOLUTION

Rorion Gracie tried everything, but nothing seemed to work. Enter former marine and ad man Arthur Davie, who took up classes with Rorion in the late 1980's. Davie was trying to marry something new to a Mexican beer label; Gracie was trying to find a new audience for jiu-jitsu. Eventually the duo hatched a plan to distribute a video series called *Gracies in Action*, one of the first "reality" series to hit any market. The tapes featured Rorion talking through the multitudes of challenge matches explaining the

techniques of what he and his family were doing. The tapes sold like hot cakes, but it wasn't until an unsuspecting article in the September 1989 issue of *Playboy* that really kick-started what Rorion was trying to accomplish.

Although karate masters had spun big tales in old martial arts rags before, the *Playboy* article gave Rorion plenty of room to banter about his challenge to anyone who thought they could champion his family's art. People showed up out of the woodwork to make the Brazilian eat his words, but it never happened. With brothers Rickson, Royce and Royler, the first Gracie Jiu-Jitsu Academy (Torrance, California) created a firestorm of activity in the martial arts world. Unlike karate and tae kwon do, the Gracies allowed their opponents to use whatever they knew in a freestyle forum of exhibition. Karate champions were tapped out by people with only a couple of months of jiu-jitsu training.

Rorion Gracie and Art Davie, along with Gracie student and Hollywood director John Milius, thought they could bring the challenge to a bigger stage. Gracie and Davie formed a company called W.O.W. Promotions for a new fight concept called War of the Worlds. They created a nice sales package, included the *Gracies in Action* tapes and the

Playboy article, but no one wanted to bite. Finally maverick cable programmer Campbell McLaren of Semapahore Entertainment Group (SEG) picked up on what Gracie and Davie already knew, and he loved the idea. The same company responsible for putting Andrew Dice Clay and Iron Maiden on pay-per-view would now test the waters with something completely different. SEG President Robert Meyrowitz signed a deal with W.O.W., the two entities researched venues and legalities, and the Ultimate Fighting Championship was born.

Though Rorion Gracie used the UFC as the best infomercial for Gracie Jiu-Jitsu, matchmaker Art Davie assembled a motley group of legitimate martial arts bad asses from karate, kung fu, and so on to compete in a one-night, winner-take-all, eight man tournament. Marketed with "There are No Rules!", the UFC debuted on November 12, 1993, and served as judge, jury and executioner of what people thought about martial arts. The years of training, the black belts, the attitudes, and some of the imposing figures meant nothing. The winner was the lanky, 6'1" Royce Gracie, who systematically tapped his opponents out with chokes and arm locks.

People at home expecting to see a real life version of *Street Fighter II* were sadly disappointed. At the same time, Royce's everyman quality gave those same people hope that size wasn't everything, and there was a more "humane" way of combat that didn't need any form of so-called brutality. SEG's marketing machine didn't help and the press picked up on a comment made by McLaren in an interview that said fights could "end by death." The pay-per-view numbers rose, but so did the controversy and the UFC became an easy political target.

MIXING IT UP

The UFC eventually got knocked off much of the pay-per-view universe that gave way to its popularity. SEG, who bought out Davie and Gracie's interest after UFC 5, added gloves, weight classes and more rules to make the sport more palatable to the naysayers led by Arizona senator John McCain. Inside the Octagon, another transformation took place. Wrestlers now shared the stage with jiu-jitsu in the grappling department; kickboxers like Maurice Smith proved their mettle with big knockouts; and wannabe tough guys were replaced by seasoned athletes who had to contend with said rules and rounds. A mixed martial artist slowly emerged, one who perhaps had a fundamental base, but was equally skilled across the board. Many point to Frank Shamrock in 1997 as being the first of his kind, but he wouldn't be alone for long.

In the late 1990's, the UFC had entered a period called the "Dark Ages" whereby only the most die-hard MMA fan knew what was going on. A lot of the PPV fans thought the show died, but thankfully because of the Internet, fandom for the sport continued to spread thanks to independent promotions around the country. The UFC's popularity also brought the sport back to Brazil in full-fledged vale tudo mode, and Japan, which promoted mixed matches in real and quasi-real form, had big money pushing a new organization called Pride Fighting Championships. Pride used a ring instead of a cage and brought more of a "show" to the fights with expensive bells and whistles, or drums, and started to build its own world class stars.

Moving into the new millennium, the UFC was running out of money and SEG honcho Bob Meyrowitz could no longer keep pumping cash into it. In January 2001, upstart Zuffa purchased the organization with UFC star Tito Ortiz' manager Dana White at the helm, and high school friends and brothers, Frank and Lorenzo Fertitta, backing the venture. Four years later, Zuffa was back on pay-per-view, in Las Vegas, but $34 million in the hole. In a last ditch effort, Zuffa agreed to buy their way on cable television with a reality show, *The Ultimate Fighter*, which was launched January 17, 2005, on brand-spanking new Spike TV. The show was a ratings bonanza that turned the UFC into a billion dollar company. Zuffa bought Pride two years later, hosts the top fighters in the world, and has opened up the promotion to a stream of merchandising that knows no limits. The sport of the future was here to stay.

ENTER MMA WORLDWIDE

Robert Pittman and Robert Pittman Jr. wanted to find a way to combine their love and admiration of the martial arts with the Pittman family business of commercial printing. Both father and son were martial artists; Pittman Sr. introduced his son to Rorion Gracie when Gracie's academy was nothing more than his garage. They followed the sport on TV and practiced on the mats, but knew an MMA-centric magazine would be a hard sell to the mainstream public.

Bodyguard Magazine made its debut in December 2004 as a way to blend the personal protection market with mixed martial arts. The full color magazine covered hand-to-hand, knife and gun defense, and included a pull-out technique section that focused on practical, effective maneuvers from personal protection experts and mixed martial artists.

After Zuffa made great strides with bringing MMA to the masses via *The Ultimate Fighter*, it was time for the publishing duo to evolve along with the sport. The following year, a trademark-licensing deal would relaunch *Bodyguard Magazine* as *TapouT Magazine*. The new name and format was just what the MMA community had been looking for, and the technique section assembled some of the best mixed martial artists to showcase their moves. A good martial artist is one who masters techniques; a great martial artist devises his own techniques.

MMA is the fastest-growing sport in the world — literally — when mixed martial artists invent new techniques and new variations the world has never seen before. In 2007, *MMA Worldwide*, a companion magazine to *TapouT Magazine*, made its debut to cover the lifestyle of the MMA world outside the cage and ring. Despite MMA gyms popping up faster than karate dojos, the Pittman's new they could always fill the void for fans and students to have easy access to techniques from the masters.

Over the years, these world class techniques have been used in and out of the gym, pulled from different issues, and traded amongst friends. For the first time, the best of the best of these expert techniques from *Bodyguard* and *TapouT* have been assembled for this special book. The techniques are equally broken out into three sections: striking, wrestling and submission.

In the striking section, some of the best trainers (Ron Van Browning and Pat Miletich, Erik Paulson) and fighters (Fedor Emelianenko, Anderson Silva, Cung Le) showcase some of their best moves. Randy Couture, Matt Lindland and Greg Nelson head up the wrestling technique section. Fans will see techniques from some of the best submission and Brazilian jiu-jitsu wizards in the world, including: Royce Gracie, Eddie Bravo, Anderson Silva, Antonio Rodrigo Nogueira, and the Machado brothers.

This action-packed book is perfect reading at home or the gym, giving the fan and the practitioner a well-rounded look at techniques that will most likely be seen in a live fight. As bi-monthly issues of *TapouT* and *MMA Worldwide Magazines* continue to hit newsstands, fans can expect future volumes to come. So move the couch, roll out the mats — be careful — and have a good time learning from the greatest mixed martial artists in the world!

Mixed martial arts is comprised of three main elements: striking, wrestling and submission. Striking, especially for new fans, is the one element most easily identified. It can be that instant "wow" factor that can end a fight as quickly as it began, or come back to haunt a fatigued fighter later in the match. Striking takes many forms: boxing, Muay Thai, traditional martial arts, ground and pound, and sometimes just plain creativity in catching a fighter off guard.

When the UFC debuted, striking wasn't a strong element. Fighting sans gloves meant that a combatant could just as easily break a hand as score damage. When David "Tank" Abbott walked into the Octagon with modified Kempo gloves and knocked out John Matua in devastating fashion, it was a sign of things to come. Gloves protect the hand — not the head — and when MMA was forced to add gloves to get back on pay-per-view, people started getting knocked out.

Kickboxer Maurice Smith was one of the first pure strikers to arrive on the scene; he made a huge impact by knocking out Brazilian jiu-jitsu stylist Conan Silveira. Thai boxer Pedro Rizzo brought power to his leg kicks

that would blacken his opponent's legs to the point they could barely walk. Vitor Belfort was a prodigy of Carlson Gracie, but his lightning fast hands could finish off his opponents before they could say jiu-jitsu. Mark Coleman came into the UFC as a wrestler, and earned the nickname "The Hammer" by controlling opponents on the mat and dazing them with his "ground and pound" technique. As for being creative, Shonie Carter took out BJJ stylist Matt Serra with not one, but two spinning backfists. When timed correctly, striking can take many forms.

As MMA evolved, wrestlers and jiu-jitsu players took up boxing, and many fighters traveled to Thailand to train in Muay Thai from the masters. Even traditional martial arts striking techniques weren't necessarily passé. Current UFC welterweight champion Georges St. Pierre was a Kyokushin karate fighter before getting into MMA. Former UFC light heavyweight champion Lyoto Machida is a karate black belt, and former UFC heavyweight champion Frank Mir was born into a traditional martial arts family.

In Brazil, even though Brazilian jiu-jitsu is the reigning style, the Chute Boxe Academy became known for its

team's striking prowess, namely in Muay Thai. Fighters from the famed academy included Wanderlei Silva, UFC middleweight champion Anderson Silva, UFC light heavyweight champion Mauricio Rua and the husband/wife team of Evangelista Santos Cyborg and current women's 145-pound champion, Cristiane Cyborg.

Strikers, win or lose, are typically the ones that get invited back because they equal excitement. It's no wonder that jiu-jitsu practitioners like BJ Penn are known to just stand and trade, or wrestler Roger Huerta will swing from the fences each and every time because that's what brings people to their feet.

The striking section includes techniques from Erik Paulson, Anderson Silva, BJ Penn and san shou stylist Cung Le. Russian sambo expert Fedor Emelianenko, kickboxing champ Kit Cope, Bas "Master of 1,000 Techniques" Rutten and trainer elite Pat Miletich also provide instruction to give students a wide range of striking techniques.

Using Your Legs

Cung Le is one of the most entertaining strikers in MMA today. His history as an undefeated San Shou fighter helped mold his dynamic striking style which includes side kicks, spinning back kicks, scissor sweeps and many more amusing techniques. Le has fought MMA exclusively for Strikeforce where he has accumulated a 7-1 record with six knockouts and was formerly the middleweight champion. His exciting striking style has led the way for a promising acting career currently starring in *Fighting* as well as several other promising endeavors on the horizon.

For more on Cung Le, log on to www.cungle.com.

Punching Combo to Body Kick

Cung is in a right handed stance squared off against an eagerly awaiting Joker who is also in a traditional stance.

Starting off with a jab, Cung gets Joker to raise his right hand in defense of the punch.

The jab is followed by a straight right hand which brings Joker's left arm up in defense.

Cung then ends his punching combo with a left hook. The hook gets Joker to continue covering up but it also allows Cung to slide to his left slightly.

With Joker covered up and not following Cung's movements, Cung takes a side step to the left.

This gives Cung distance to throw a body kick from Joker's side.

With Joker's hands up protecting his face, this opens up Joker's entire midsection for a kick.

A master of Kung-Fu San Soo under the legendary Jimmy Woo, Ron Van Browning is an expert in real combat tactics and has trained top bodyguards, SWAT members, FBI agents, DEA operatives, Golden Glove boxers, and UFC fighters. "In a combative situation," says Van Browning, "you have to use all aspects of the martial arts. You don't necessarily want to hurt someone, but you want to put yourself into a position of command and control just in case your opponent escalates the encounter and you have to respond in like manner for self-preservation." In this series of moves, Van Browning shows how a synthesis of the grappling and striking arts can be used to gain an advantage in a variety of physical encounters.

Right-Hook Counterstrike Combination...

Ron Van Browning faces UFC champion Matt Hughes.

As Hughes throws a right hook, Van Browning blocks it with his left hand...

...punches Hughes' left thigh to get him to bend forward...

...and follows with a right uppercut to the chin.

Van Browning then turns his body to load his right arm...

...and then finishes with a right elbow to the head.

With a record of 29-7-2, Pat Miletich "The Croation Sensation" is one of the world's most experienced and respected fighters. The list of his "victims" reads like a Who's Who of MMA fighting and includes such world-class athletes as Shonie Carter, Andre Pederneiras, Jorge Patino, Chris Brennan, and Townsend Saunders. As well known as he is as a fighter, however, Miletich has established an even greater reputation as a trainer and coach for Team Miletich, the single most feared fighting academy in the world, which boasts such stars as Matt Hughes, Robbie Lawler, Tim Sylvia, Jeremy Horn, and others. A competent grappler, Miletich is admittedly most explosive on his feet, where he can deliver punishment with the hands, elbows, knees, or feet. "A complete fighter has to know how to strike," says Miletich. "Grappling specialists just don't last very long in the Octagon anymore."

Left-Hook Block and Counter...

Pat Miletich squares-up with opponent Matt Hughes.

As Hughes throws a left hook, Miletich brings up his right hand to block the punch, like he is combing his hair, while simultaneously turning his body to cock his left hand.

He then counterpunches to Hughes' chin.

Left-Hook Block, Right-Cross Counter...

Pat Miletich faces opponent Matt Hughes.

As Hughes throws a left hook, Miletich brings up his right hand to block the punch, like he is combing his hair, while leaning forward to make the punch miss his face if it lands.

Miletich then counters with a right cross to Hughes' chin.

SEE PAGE 176 FOR AN EXCLUSIVE MMA WORLDWIDE PACKAGE DEAL!

Close-In Striking

Right-Cross Counter...

Pat Miletich faces opponent Matt Hughes.

As Hughes throws a right cross, Miletich turns his body, left shoulder forward, and lets the punch go by as he cocks his right hand.

Miletich then unleashes a right cross to Hughes' chin.

Kneeing to the Body...

Pat Miletich clinches Matt Hughes around the neck, making Hughes bring his arms down to block.

Miletich then brings his right knee up...

...and pushes his hips forward and pulls Hughes towards him (note how Pat's knee sneaks under Hughes' block to hit him in the stomach).

As Hughes responds by blocking the knees with his arms...

...Miletich brings his knee up, in front of his arms...

...pushes his hips forward while pulling Hughes' head down, and knees him in the face.

With a string of victories in KOTC against only one defeat, Nam Phan seems destined to become an NHB star. "He has all the qualities you like to see in a young fighter," says KOTC headman Terry Trebilcock. "He's explosive, unpredictable, knows how to grapple, and has heavy hands. I expect great things from him in the future." A wrestler at Goldenwest College before turning to cagefighting, Phan has combined Brazilian jiu-jitsu submissions with wrestling takedowns and boxing hands to become a complete and dangerous fighter. Phan has also managed to combine the two cultures of America and South Vietnam and is the pride of "Little Saigon" in Southern California. "As one of the few Vietnamese fighters in NHB, I feel a special responsibility to do well," Phan says. "It isn't so much about winning or losing, but rather about knowing that you did your absolute best. Although the connection between the U.S. and South Vietnam occurred before I was born, I always remember my roots and I never forget how much America sacrificed for the people of South Vietnam. So when I enter the cage to fight I always have the flags of America and South Vietnam with me."

Knee-Strike Clinch Defense

Nam Phan squares off against author Bobby Pittman.

Bobby comes in and tries to clinch with Nam.

Nam brings his right arm over Bobby's left arm, forces it down, and pulls Bobby's left hand off his neck.

Nam does the same thing with his left arm – successfully taking both of Bobby's arms off his neck.

Nam grabs the back of Bobby's neck to work his own clinch.

Nam finishes by pulling Bobby's head down and landing a knee to the face.

Knee-Strike Single-Leg Defense

Nam Phan and Bobby Pittman square off.

Bobby shoots in and gets a single leg on Nam's right leg.

Nam posts his left hand on Bobby's head and pushes it away. With his right hand, Nam reaches under Bobby's left arm and grabs his own wrist for a three-quarter nelson.

Nam sprawls his legs back and drops his weight on Bobby's head. This forces Bobby's head into the ground and causes him to lose his grip on Nam's leg.

Nam finishes with a left knee to Bobby's head. In order for Bobby to escape, he must let go of Nam's leg – which is exactly what Nam wants.

Anderson "The Spider" Silva is arguably the best striker in Mixed Martial Arts today. The UFC middleweight champion has beat all 11 opponents he has faced in the UFC and has knocked out seven of them, including Nate Marquardt, Travis Lutter and Rich Franklin twice. His unorthodox and technical Muay Thai is feared by the entire middleweight division. Look for Silva to continue to test the light heavyweight division after his impressive KO over former belt holder, Forrest Griffin.

These techniques are from Anderson Silva's New Victory Belt book *Mixed Martial Arts Instruction Manuel: Striking.*

Blinding Hand / Reverse Elbow

Feijao and Anderson are squared off.

Anderson elevates his right arm and extends it toward Feijao's face.

As he extends his right arm, he opens his hand and positions his palm directly in front of Feijao's face momentarily blocking his vision.

Using the opening created by his feint, Anderson steps his right foot forward and plants it to the inside of Feijao's left foot. At the same time he drops his right arm, slightly turn his body in a counterclockwise direction, and chambers his right elbow by moving his right arm across my body.

Driving his hips and weight forward, Anderson throws his right elbow upward between Feijao's guard and strike his chin.

SEE PAGE 176 FOR AN EXCLUSIVE MMA WORLDWIDE PACKAGE DEAL!

Counter Jab with Spinning Back Elbow

Feijao and Anderson are in southpaw stances.

Feijao throws a right jab at Anderson's face. To evade his punch, Anderson parries his fist toward his right side using his left hand and slips his head towards his left side.

As Feijao's fist sails by the side of his head, Anderson steps his right foot to the outside of Feijao's lead leg. Notice he is coming down on the ball of his foot.

Still rotating his body in a counterclockwise direction, Anderson drops his right heel to the mat and distributes a larger portion of his weight onto his right leg.

Continuing to rotate his body in a counterclockwise direction, Anderson pivots on his right foot, slides his left foot toward Feijao's right foot, and throws his left elbow straight back into his chin.

7 Counters to a Right Cross

with **Erik Paulson**

Erik Paulson is a former two-time world Shooto champion who was the first American to win a Shooto title in Japan. Defending the title for 9 years, Erik became the first superstar of the Shooto world. He now travels the world giving Shooto, grappling, and martial arts seminars and recently opened a new school, Orange County Shootwrestling, in southern California. Here he shows a few of his favorite techniques.

For more information on seminars or classes with Erik Paulson, or on his complete line of training DVDs, visit www.erikpaulson.com.

Counter the Right Cross with a Right Cross

Erik is squared off with his opponent Dave.

Dave throws a right cross at Erik's head. Erik takes a small step to the left a slips his head outside the punch.

Erik counters with a right cross.

Counter the Right Cross with a Right Knee

Erik is squared off with Dave.

Dave throws a right cross at Erik's head. Erik steps to the left, outside of the punch. Erik uses his forearms to push Dave's arm away.

Erik grabs the back of Dave's head with his right hand and pulls down as he throws a right knee to Dave's midsection.

7 Counters to a Right Cross

with **Erik Paulson**

Counter the Right Cross with a Left Hook to the Body (Option 1)

Erik is squared off with Dave.

Dave throws a right cross at Erik's head. Erik twists his body to the left to slip outside the punch. Notice how this sets Erik up for the left hook.

Erik counters with a left hook to Dave's body.

Counter the Right Cross with a Left Hook to the Body (Option 2)

Erik is squared off with Dave.

Dave throws a right cross at Erik's head. Erik bends his legs and slips underneath the punch. Notice how Erik also loads his left hand for the hook.

Erik counters with a left hook to the body.

Counter the Right Cross with a Left Uppercut

Erik is squared off with Dave.

Dave throws a right cross at Erik's head. Erik twists his body and slips outside the punch.

Erik counters with a left uppercut to Dave's chin.

Counter the Right Cross with an Overhand Right

Erik is squared off with Dave.

Dave throws a right cross at Erik's head. Erik twists his body and slips outside the punch.

Erik counters with an overhand right to Dave's head.

Counter the Right Cross with a Right Low Kick

Erik is squared off with Dave.

Dave throws a right cross at Erik's head. Erik steps to the left and twists his body to slip outside the punch. Notice how Erik uses his left forearm to push the punch away.

Erik pivots on his left foot and brings his right leg up for the kick.

Here you can see how Erik brings his leg up...

...and finishes with the low kick on Dave's left thigh.

Val Leedy is the kickboxing instructor at United Mixed Martial Arts in La Mirada, CA. Val has trained in many different styles under such greats as Erik Paulson, Kru Rex, Hector Gonzales, Eddy Millis, Jay Martinez and too many more to list. When he's not teaching, Val can be found fighting in MMA and kickboxing matches around the world as well as promoting his own events. For more info on Val and training with him visit the UMMA website at www.unitedmixedmartialarts.com or visit the school at 15843 East Imperial Highway, La Mirada, CA 90638.

Counter to an Overhand Right

Val is squared off against Jay Martinez.

Jay throws a big overhand right a Val's head. Val steps forward with his left foot, and jams the punch with his left forearm.

With his left arm, Val reaches under Jay's right arm for the under hook. With his right, Val reaches around Jay's neck and locks his hands for the head and arm control.

Here you can see how Val has his right arm around Jay's neck. Notice how Val keeps his elbow down and against Jay's chest.

Val pulls down with his right arm and pushes up with his left arm to get Jay off balance and expose Jay's body on his right side.

Now, Val throws a knee to Jay's body. From here, Val can stay in the clinch and continue to knee, he can back away, or he can go for the takedown.

Check out the brand new

Vicious Strikers

Counter to an Overhand Right

Val is squared off against Jay Martinez.

Jay throws a big overhand right a Val's head. Val steps forward with his left foot, and jams the punch with his left forearm.

Val steps forward with his right leg and gets an under hook with his right arm. Val also wraps his left arm around Jay's right arm for the over hook.

Here you can see how Val has the over-under on Jay.

Val twists his body to the left and bumps Jay back with his right shoulder.

Here you can see how Val bumped Jay back with his right shoulder to create space between them. This gives Val room to strike.

Val brings his left arm up...

...and finishes with an elbow to Jay's face.

If you're a gym owner call us about **Gym Association**

Striking Combos

Counter to a One-Two

Emerson, known as The Saint, is a former Pancrase and King of the Cage fighter. He was a cast member of *The Ultimate Fighter 5* and has fought his last 7 fights in the UFC. He holds a 9-9 record with 1 no contest. He fights out of No Limits in Irvine, CA and trains with some other top talent including Aaron Witherspoon, Bao Quach, Tim Persey and Juliano Prado.

Robert and Bobby are squared off (both are right handed.)

Bobby throws a jab with his left so Robert turns his hips and blocks with his right elbow covering his head.

Bobby follows the jab with a right straight so Robert turns his hips the opposite direction and blocks the same way but with his left arm.

Robert turns his hips into Bobby delivering a right hook (notice Robert is still protecting his face with his left hand.)

Robert follows it up with a left hook to the body.

He finishes with a right leg kick.

Striking Combos

Striking Combo Counter to a Leg Kick

Bobby and Robert are squared off.

Bobby throws a right leg kick so Robert checks the kick.

Robert then immediately steps in and delivers a jab.

Robert then throws a straight right...

...then a left uppercut.

Robert rotates his body...

...and delivers a spinning elbow.

Striking Combos

Counter to a Countered Jab

Bobby and Robert are squared off.

Robert delivers a jab that is parried by Bobby.

Bobby delivers a hook off of the parried jab.

Robert blocks the hook by covering with his elbow and arm and rotating his body to the left.

Robert then delivers a left uppercut...

...and finishes with a right knee.

Raising the Bar on Nutrition www.2to1proteinbars.com

Striking Combos

Elbows and Knees Combo from a Jab

Bobby and Robert are squared off.

Robert throws a left jab.

Robert clears Bobby's left arm with his right hand.

Robert then uses that space to throw a right elbow.

With the same angle, Robert controls Bobby's neck with his right hand and throws a right knee to the body.

Robert finishes with a left elbow to the head.

Ian Harris is the head trainer and founder of Fight Science MMA Fight Team, based out of Los Angeles, California. Ian began his training in boxing at the age of 6. At age 13, Ian began training in the martial arts in Kenpo, Muay Thai, Jeet Kune Do Concepts and Shooto, before beginning Brazilian Jiu Jitsu in 1996. In 2003 Ian began teaching his own version of Mixed Martial Arts based on his 25 Plus years of experience, which he calls Fight Science. That same year he and a partner also started the MMA Clothing and apparel company, PsyK.O. Gear. For more info, visit www.fightsciencemma.com and www.psykogear.com.

American PsyKO

Julian Rush has Ian in side control with an 'over-under' grip.

Ian hooks his left ankle with his left wrist pulling it as high as he can past Julian's head, keeping a tight space with his elbow.

Pushing his knee in with his left arm to keep the tight space, Ian grabs his ankle with his right hand now.

Ian triangles his legs trapping the head and isolating Julian's right arm, still pushing on the knee to eliminate space for Julian's head to escape.

Julian fears the arm bar, so he cross faces Ian in order to free his right arm.

Ian grabs Julian's left wrist and reaches over the elbow looking for the Americana.

Ian grabs his wrist and finishes with the Americana on Julian's left arm.

The Hex

Chad George is in Ian's guard.

Ian overhooks Chad's right arm for control and to keep Chad from punching.

Opening the guard, Ian puts his left foot on Chad's hip and pushes Chad's head away with his right hand, keeping the overhook on the arm.

Here is the position from the reverse angle. Pushing on the head creates space and keeps Chad from striking with his left hand as well.

Ian slides his right leg underneath Chad's left arm, threading it between Chad's arm and his head.

Ian releases the overhook to grab his ankle with his left hand, pulling tight to keep Chad from sitting up and squeezing down with his left knee on Chad's ribs.

As Ian tightens up the position he punches to keep Chad from trying to sit up and escape. As Chad burries his head to avoid getting hit, Ian locks the position tighter.

Ian now rolls from his side to his back, scooting his hips back under Chad and locks in the triangle. He continues punching to keep Chad's head down.

Since Ian does not have Chad's arm across his body and is more square to Chad than with a typical triangle choke, Ian reaches behind his own knee with his right arm and behind Chad's head with his left arm and uses the Gable grip to squeeze and get the submission.

A different angle shows how the pressure is applied a bit different with The Hex than with a standard triangle. Ian squeezes all points to the center by getting as compact as he can.

Gizzard From Thai Clinch

Ian has Chad George in a Thai Clinch.

Ian overhooks Chad's arm with his left arm, maintaining control on Chad's neck with his right hand.

Ian switches his stance to the side, using both hands to push on Chad's head, retaining control on Chad's right arm.

Ian now delivers a knee to Chad's head.

Keeping his control on Chad's head with his left hand and overhook, Ian releases his right hand and moves back in front of Chad.

Keeping Chad's head firmly on his stomach, Ian reaches his right arm deep.

The reverse angle shows Ian as he reaches his right arm and grabs his left elbow.

Keeping his hips underneath him and Chad's head on his stomach, Ian arches his back and drives his forearm into Chad's throat for the Gizzard choke. Note that the left hand stays on the back of Chad's head with overhook intact.

Swim & Sink

Ian has Julian Rush in his Thai Clinch.

Julian begins to swim his left arm to get an underhook.

Ian releases his grip with his right hand and turns completely perpendicular to Julian, letting Julian's arm reach. By turning as far away as he can, Ian does not allow Julian to get the underhook.

Ian delivers an elbow to Julian's head. He can also punch.

After striking, Ian re-establishes his clinch.

Julian looks to get an underhook again. The reverse angle shows how Ian maintains control of Julian's head with his left hand keeping his left elbow very tight to Julian's chest.

If your opponent sees the strike coming, he will cover his face, as Julian does in this frame to block the strike.

So Ian abandons the strike and checks Julian's elbow pushing it in and moving toward Julian's back.

Ian now has Julian's back and can throw, choke or move the fight forward as he pleases from this position.

See bio on page 20.

Knees to the Body in the Clinch

Anderson and his opponent are squared off.

Anderson takes a short step in with his right foot and brings his right arm inside his opponent's left arm.

He reaches for a collar tie with his right hand...

...and finishes the Thai clinch with his left hand.

Anderson then drops his hips bringing his opponent's head down.

His opponent is now open for a left knee to the body. Notice Anderson's toe is pointed down and his hips have exploded forward.

After the knee strike Anderson drops his left foot inside his opponent's left foot.

Pushing forward with his forearms, Anderson creates more space so he can...

...deliver a knee with his other leg.

Knee Pressure in the Thai Clinch

Anderson has his opponent's hips bent using the Thai clinch.

With his opponent in an awkward position Anderson can knee strike to the body or face.

Here is a look at another angle.

Anderson drops his shin after the knee strike into his opponent's shin.

Pushing his knee into his opponent's knee he can get him off balance.

Now Anderson can throw another knee to the body.

Knees and Elbows

More Cool Knee Strikes

1 Anderson has a collar tie with his left hand and controlling his opponent's far wrist.

2 Anderson passes his opponent's left arm across his body and grips his opponent's left tricep with his left hand.

3 Now Anderson cups the right side of his opponent's head and pulls his head into a knee strike to the kidneys.

1 Anderson just caught a body kick to his side.

2 Reaching across with his right hand Anderson grips his opponent's right lat.

3 Pulling down with his right hand, Anderson can knee his opponent's body.

1 Anderson is controlling his opponent's right arm with his left and has a collar tie with his right.

2 Pushing with his right arm, Anderson gets his opponent off balance.

3 Now Anderson can sneak his right knee into the face of his opponent through his two arms.

More Cool Elbow Strikes

1

Anderson and his opponent are squared off.

2

His opponent throws a right hook so Anderson protects his head with his left elbow and arm.

3

Anderson turns his hips into his opponent and delivers an elbow to the face.

1

Anderson's opponent throws a jab so Anderson creates distance with a front kick.

2

Dropping his lead leg to his right, Anderson briefly turns his back to his opponent...

3

...then delivers a spinning back elbow to his opponent's face.

1

Anderson's opponent throws a right straight so Anderson rotates his body away from the strike.

2

Anderson then takes a step inside with his right foot...

3

and delivers a devastating up elbow.

Hawaii native BJ Penn is one of the most dangerous fighters in the lightweight division. Currently ranked #2 in the MMA Worldwide Lightweight Rankings, Penn has defeated the likes of Takanori Gomi, Matt Serra, Renzo Gracie and Matt Hughes. The first non-Brazilian to win the Brazilian Jiu Jitsu World Championships, Penn is dangerous not only in submissions but in wrestling and striking as well. Here are three displays of his well rounded techniques.

"This is from BJ Penn's best-selling martial arts book, 'Mixed Martial Arts: The Book of Knowledge.' It is available at Budovideos.com and bookstores everywhere."

Slip Cross to 3 Punch Combo

BJ is squared off with Albert in the pocket.

Albert throws a right cross at BJ's face so he slips his punch by rotating his hips and shoulders in a counterclockwise direction and leaning slightly to his left. Notice how slipping the cross loads BJ's hips up for the body hook.

With Albert's right arm extended, his ribs are vulnerable on his right side. BJ takes advantage of this by rotating his hips in a clockwise direction and hammering a hook to his body.

Before Albert has a chance to recover, BJ prepares to throw a left uppercut straight up the middle.

The uppercut collides with Albert's chin, lifting his head up and exposing his jaw for the right cross.

BJ finishes the counter combination by rotating his hips in a counterclockwise direction and throwing a right cross to Albert's jaw.

SEE PAGE 176 FOR AN EXCLUSIVE MMA WORLDWIDE PACKAGE DEAL!

Striking to Arm Bar

BJ is in the mount position. Opening his left hand, he drives the 'V' between his thumb and fingers into Beach's neck. To strangle him, BJ locks his left arm straight and drives his weight down into Beach's neck.

BJ cocks his right hand back to drop a punch to Beach's face.

Keeping Beach's head pinned to the mat with his left hand, he drops his fist into Beach's left eye.

As BJ brings his right hand back to throw another strike, Beach extends both arms in an attempt to block the anticipated blow.

The moment Beach extends his arms, BJ posts his left foot on the mat, rotates his hips in a counterclockwise direction, and drops his right arm to trap Beach's left arm to his chest.

Dropping his weight onto Beach, BJ steps his right leg over Beach's head and sits down on his left shoulder. Notice BJ has his hips below Beach's elbow keeping Beach from escaping.

As BJ starts to fall down to his back, he wraps his right arm around Beach's left arm to secure it to his chest.

Keeping his legs coiled tight, BJ falls all the way down to his back and latches onto Beach's left arm with both hands. After making sure Beach's left thumb is pointing toward the ceiling, BJ finishes the submission by squeezing his knees together, pulling Beach's arm towards his chest with both hands, and elevates his hips.

Punching Your Leg Free

1 Reagan has BJ in a single leg. Notice BJ has his left foot wedged in between Reagan's legs for balance.

2 Balancing on his right leg, BJ controls Reagan's head with his left arm and drives a right uppercut into his left eye socket.

3 He winds up for another uppercut...

4 ...and yet another uppercut to Reagan's left eye socket.

5 Blind and frustrated, Reagan loosens his grip on BJ's left leg. Immediately, BJ maneuvers his head to the right side of Reagan's head, stripping him of the positioning he needs to finish the single-leg takedown.

6 Bringing his elbows in tight to his body and pinching Reagan's arms together with his hands, BJ regains his base and postures and drives his left leg to the ground.

7 Although he has escaped the single-leg, BJ continues to push Reagan's arms together with his hands to avoid getting punched as he backs out.

8 Backing away, BJ continues to control Reagan's arms to avoid getting hit. From here he will return to his standard fighting stance and begin to set up an attack.

With an MMA record of 30-8-0, Quinton Jackson has definitely established himself as one of the greatest fighters in the world at the 205 lb. weight class. Hailing from Memphis, Tennessee, Jackson now resides in Southern California. Jackson comes from a wrestling background and it definitely shows. In a fight with Ricardo Arona, Jackson showed his brutal power by slamming Arona hard enough for a knockout victory. It's this style that makes "Rampage" one of the most exciting fighters to watch, so check him out. Here he shows some of his favorite ways to finish a fight.

Striking Combo

Jackson starts the combo with a left jab to the head.

He then follows the jab with a right cross.

The two punches push his opponent back, putting him in perfect range for a leg kick. Jackson throws an inside leg kick with his left leg.

He then finishes the combo with a right elbow to the head.

The Basics of Boxing

DG Boxing, located in Long Beach, California, is home to countless championship boxers, both amateur and professional, as well as a cardio boxing gym. MMA fighters such as Tito Ortiz and Tank Abbott have trained at DG Boxing through out their careers.

Dorian Anthony is a four time Los Angeles Golden Gloves Champion, 2008 USA Boxing National Champion, 2007 National PAL Champion and the 2007 BCR World Champion earning himself a #1 ranking by USA Boxing. With his sights set on the 2012 Summer Olympics in London, look for Dorian to make a splash in years to come.

Having trained since he was 9 years old, George Rodriguez brings over 20 years of experience to the DG Boxing gym. A Golden Gloves winner as well as a Diamond Belt Tournament Champion as an amateur, George also boasts an 11-1 professional record. Having been with DG Boxing for four years now, he is one of the head trainers at the gym.

For more on DG Boxing log on to www.dgboxinggyms.com

Five Counters to a Jab

Both fighters are right handed boxers. Dorian (right) throws a jab. George drops his level and jabs at the midsection of Dorian.

George drops his level and throws a right straight at the midsection of Dorian.

George slips to his left and throws an over hand right to Dorian's head.

George slips to his left and throws a left uppercut.

George blocks with his right hand and throws a jab with his left.

Combo Off a Jab Defense

George and Dorian are squared off.

Dorian throws a jab which George immediately parries with his right hand.

Immediately after George closes the distance and throws a right hand to the chin.

Followed by a left hook to the head.

And finishing with another right straight.

SEE PAGE 176 FOR AN EXCLUSIVE MMA WORLDWIDE PACKAGE DEAL!

Combo Off a Right Straight Defense

George and Dorian are squared off.

George throws a straight right to Dorian's head. Dorian brings his glove up to his cheek and turns his hips slightly to the right to block the punch.

Dorian now turns his hips back toward George and throws a right straight to George's face.

Taking a step forward and out with his right foot, Dorian throws a left hook to George's face.

Followed by a right hook to the head.

Countering Hooks

George and Dorian are squared off.

George throws a right hook to Dorian's head so he lifts his left glove up to his head to block . . .

. . . and counters with a left jab.

George throws a left hook to Dorian's head so he lifts his right glove up to his head to block . . .

. . . and counters with a right straight.

George throws a left hook to Dorian's body so Dorian tilts his body to the right and brings his right arm close to his body to block . . .

. . . and counters with a right uppercut.

George throws a right hook to Dorian's body so Dorian tilts his body to the left and brings his left arm close to his body to block . . .

. . . and counters with a left uppercut.

Combo Defense Off an Uppercut

1

George and Dorian are squared off.

2

George throws a left uppercut but Dorian blocks the punch with his left hand pushing George's punching hand down.

3

This leaves George's head wide open so Dorian throws a straight right.

4

Dorian then follows with a left hook to the head . . .

5

. . . and finishes with a straight right.

DG Boxing, located in Long Beach, California, is home to countless championship boxers, both amateur and professional, as well as a cardio boxing gym. MMA fighters such as Tito Ortiz and Tank Abbott have trained at DG Boxing throughout their careers.

Dorian Anthony is a four time Los Angeles Golden Gloves Champion, 2008 USA Boxing National Champion, 2007 National PAL Champion and the 2007 BCR World Champion earning himself a #1 ranking by USA Boxing. With his sights set on the 2012 Summer Olympics in London, look for Dorian to make a splash in years to come.

Having trained since he was 9 years old, Jorge Rodriguez brings over 20 years of experience to the DG Boxing gym. A Golden Gloves winner as well as a Diamond Belt Tournament Champion as an amateur, George also boasts an 11-1 professional record. Having been with DG Boxing for four years now, he is one of the head trainers at the gym.

For more on DG Boxing log on to www.dgboxinggyms.com

Uppercut Counter

Jorge (left) and Dorian are two right handed fighters squared off.

Jorge throws a right uppercut so Dorian blocks by rotating his body counter clockwise placing his hand, palm down, under his chin blocking the punch.

With his body already rotated and Jorge's right hand away from his face, Dorian rotates his shoulders and throws a left hook to Jorge's chin.

Dorian follows up with a straight right.

Using Your Legs

Cung Le is one of the most entertaining strikers in MMA today. His history as an undefeated San Shou fighter helped mold his dynamic striking style which includes side kicks, spinning back kicks, scissor sweeps and many more amusing techniques. Le has fought MMA exclusively for Strikeforce where he has accumulated a 6-1 record with six knockouts and was formerly the middleweight champion. His exciting striking style has led the way for a promising acting career currently starring in *Fighting* as well as several other promising endeavors on the horizon.

For more on Cung Le, log on to www.cungle.com.

Spinning Back Kick

Cung is in an orthodox stance squared off with Joker.

He throws a jab to distract his opponent.

Making sure he is in a set stance before he makes his moves, Cung brings his jab hand back into position.

The brief second where Joker is distracted by the jab allows Cung time to get his hips into position. He takes a short step to the right with his lead leg.

Now Cung pushes off his back foot and rotates on his front foot spinning his head around first so he can see what he is going to strike. His right leg follows.

Cung pushes his right foot straight into the bag finishing the kick.

 ZEBRA MATS www.ZebraMats.com

50

Front Side Kick

Cung is squared off in a left handed fighter's stance.

Bringing his left foot in next to his right foot gives Cung the space he needs to stretch out and reach his opponent.

Cung brings his right knee straight up into his chest, cocking his foot for the strike.

He then stretches his foot into the chest of his opponent.

Punching Combo to Body Kick

Cung is in a right handed stance squared off against an eagerly awaiting Joker who is also in a traditional stance.

Starting off with a jab, Cung gets Joker to raise his right hand in defense of the punch.

The jab is followed by a straight right hand which brings Joker's left arm up in defense.

Cung then ends his punching combo with a left hook. The hook gets Joker to continue covering up but it also allows Cung to slide to his left slightly.

With Joker covered up and not following Cung's movements, Cung takes a side step to the left.

This gives Cung distance to throw a body kick from Joker's side.

With Joker's hands up protecting his face, this opens up Joker's entire midsection for a kick.

Flying Roundhouse Kick

Cung is in a right handed stance.

Keeping his hands up in defense, Cung drops his hips and puts his weight on his front foot.

Cung brings his right arm up and begins pushing off his back leg ready to take flight.

Pulling his right arm down while pushing off his feet gets Cung airborne while also rotating his body to increase the power delivered by the kick. Notice Cung's back leg is still trailing.

To finish the strike, Cung whips his hips and shin forward into his opponent.

Fedor Emelianenko is quite simply the best. The former Pride heavyweight champion and current WAMMA champion has been one of the most complete fighters of the last ten years. His power punches and unorthodox boxing have made many a heavyweight his victim in Russia, Japan and the US. His KO victims include Andrei Arlovski, Tsuyoshi Kohsaka and Gary Goodridge.

THIS TECHNIQUE IS FROM FEDOR'S NEW VICTORY BELT BOOK, *FEDOR: THE FIGHTING SYSTEM OF THE WORLD'S UNDISPUTED KING OF MMA. To purchase, go to www.victorybelt.com.*

Body Uppercut to Left Hook

Kirill and Fedor are fighting in close range. Fedor keeps both hands up to protect my head.

Fedor spring-loads his hips and shoulders by corkscrewing his body in a counterclockwise direction and dipping his head toward his left side.

Fedor whips his hips and shoulders in a clockwise direction, pivots on his left foot, and throws a left uppercut to Kirill's abdomen.

Landing the left uppercut to Kirill's body causes him to dip toward his right side. To capitalize on this opening, Fedor rotates his hips and shoulders in a counterclockwise direction and prepares to throw a left hook at the right side of Kirill's head.

Fedor whips his hips and shoulders in a clockwise direction, pivots on his left foot, and throws a left hook at the right side of Kirill's face. From here, Fedor can continue throwing strikes, execute a takedown, or tie him up in the clinch.

Lead Inside Hand Trap to Right Cross

Fedor is in his fighting stance, searching for an opening to attack.

To break Kirill's guard and create an opening for a right cross, Fedor slaps Kirill's left arm away from his body using his left arm. Notice how Fedor slaps the inside of his arm instead of the top.

As Kirill's guard is forced open, Fedor rotates his hips and shoulders in a counterclockwise direction, pivots on the ball of his right foot, draws his left arm back into his stance, and throws a right cross at Kirill's exposed face.

Lead Outside Hand Trap to Straight Cross

Kirill is standing in a southpaw stance and Fedor Is standing in a traditional fighting stance.

To break Kirill's guard and setup the cross, Fedor steps his left foot to the outside of Kirill's right foot and places his left hand against the outside of Kirill's right hand.

Fedor slaps Kirill's right hand down and to the inside of Kirill's body using his left arm.

Having opened Kirill's guard, Fedor rotates his hips and shoulders in a counterclockwise direction, pivots on the ball of his right foot, draws his left hand back into his stance, and throws a right cross toward Kirill's face.

Continuing to rotate his hips and shoulders in a counterclockwise direction and pivot on the ball of his right foot, Fedor lands a straight right cross to Kirill's face. From here, Fedor will capitalize on Kirill's stunned state by following up with another attack.

Former Pride heavyweight champion has been the hands down best heavyweight fighter for years. One of the most dominant, if not the most dominant, MMA fighters in history did most of his damage with brutal striking that set up classic Sambo takedowns and submissions. With a list of victims that include Antonio Rodrigo Nogueira, Mirko "Cro Cop", Mark Hunt and Mark Coleman, just to name a few, he is looking to add another victim to his list in former UFC champion Tim Sylvia in Affliction's debut show Banned on July 19th. This technique is from Victory Belt's new book, Fedor: The Fighting System of the World's Undisputed King of MMA. It will be available wherever books are sold. *To purchase online, go to www.victorybelt.com.*

Counter Cross to 3 Punch Combo

Fedor is in his fighting stance, searching for an opening to attack.

His opponent rotates his hips in a counterclockwise direction and begins throwing his right hand. Reading his movements, Fedor begins to slip his right cross by dipping his head to his left side and rotating his hips and shoulders in a counterclockwise direction.

Continuing to rotate his hips and shoulders in a counterclockwise direction, Fedor drops his level by bending at the knees and throws a straight right cross to his opponent's solar plexus.

The instant Fedor lands the right cross to his opponent's body, Fedor rotates his hips and shoulders in a clockwise direction and prepares to throw a left uppercut at his face.

In order to acquire the angle needed to land the left uppercut, Fedor takes a small step forward with his right foot. At the same time, he rotates his hips and shoulders in a clockwise direction, pulls his right hand back into his stance, and throws a left uppercut at his opponent's chin.

The impact of the uppercut forces his opponent to take a step backward.

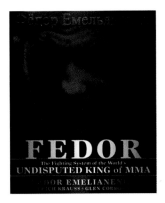

Fedor continues by stepping his left foot forward, rotating his hips and shoulders in a counterclockwise direction, pulling his left hand back into his stance, and throwing a right cross at opponent's head.

Kit Cope is an accomplished Muay Thai fighter and an MMA veteran but is probably better known for his television accolades. Cope has appeared on *Fear Factor*, MTV's *Real Life* and as one of three hosts on SpikeTV's *Wild World of Sports*. Having traveled to Thailand to train and compete, Cope is well versed in Muay Thai with dangerous punches, knees, kicks and elbows.

Left Hook Counter to Knee

Kit and his opponent are squared off.

His opponent throws a wide left hook to Kit's head so Kit blocks by putting his right hand behind his neck and blocking with his elbow.

Safe from the punch, Kit grips his opponent's shoulders and takes a step forward with his right foot.

A closer look on his grip shows Kit's right hand on his opponent's left bicep and his left hand on the back of his neck pushing his head down.

From here Kit leans back, shoots his hips forward and lands a knee to the sternum.

Muay Thai Counters

with **Mark DellaGrotte**

Mark DellaGrotte is one of the most respected trainers in MMA today. Specializing in Muay Thai kickboxing at his Sityodtong Gym in Somerville, Massachusetts, DellaGrotte has trained the likes of Kenny Florian, Frank Mir, Stephan Bonnar, Marcus Davis, Jorge Rivera and Patrick Côté

Before becoming an MMA coach, before becoming one of the few "farang" (foreigner) to earn a ranking at Bangkok's Rajdamnern Stadium, Mark DellaGrotte was just a kid from Boston with a passion for Muay Thai. This passion led him to Thailand and to nights on concrete floors in rural gyms and vicious ring fights, all in order to live and train in the traditional Thai way.

For more on Mark DellaGrotte, log on to www.sityodtong.com.

Photos by Daniel Rauch

Leg Sweep

Plasma fires a jab . . .

. . . which Mark parries with his left hand.

Plasma then follows up with a body kick with his right leg.

Mark captures the kick with his left arm.

With the leg secure, Mark takes a step forward with his left leg.

Now moving with his momentum forward, Mark posts his right hand on Plasma, starts to kick with his right leg . . .

. . . and hits Plasma's left leg knocking him to the ground.

Body Kick Counter

Mark and Plasma are squared off.

Plasma throws a body kick with his right leg.

Mark steps laterally with his right leg away from the force of the kick looking to catch the leg.

With the leg secure, mark plants his feet.

Now Mark can throw a straight right to the face of Plasma.

Then finishes the combination by pulling Plasma's shoulder and delivering a knee.

Muay Thai Counters

Body Kick Counter to Upper Cut

Mark, in a right handed stance, is squared off with Plasma, in a left handed stance.

Plasma lifts his front leg as if attempting a teep (push kick).

Instead, Plasma plants his lead foot and throws a body kick with his back leg.

Mark sees the kick coming . . .

. . . so he closes the distance and turns his body so the strike hits his shoulder and plants his lead leg.

Now Mark is in good position to throw an uppercut . . .

. . . to the chin of Plasma.

Scott Smith is one of the most durable and tough strikers in MMA. His background in Muay Thai coupled with one of the sturdiest chins in MMA has helped him rack up 17 wins, 14 by KO. The middleweight, currently signed with Strikeforce, has had many memorable battles, mostly striking. Some notable comebacks include wins over Pete Sell, Benji Radach and Cung Le, all wins by KO. Smith should never be counted out of any fight he is in.

Photos by Dan Rauch

Fake Right to Left Hook

Scott and Plasma are squared off. Scott in a right handed stance and Plasma in a left handed stance.

Scott pretends to throw a straight right by turning his right shoulder to his opponent. This sets up the left hook.

With his body already cocked for a left hook, he is able to deliver the powerful punch.

Rotating the opposite direction, Scott can now throw a right straight. Notice Scott was rotating on his hips and toes with every punch.

Side Kick Defense

Scott and Plasma are squared off.

Plasma "chambers" his leg to throw a side kick to Scott's body.

As the kick comes towards Scott, he rotates his upper body clockwise and brings his arms in.

Scott tightens his core allowing the kick to hit his forearm instead of his body.

Side Kick Counter

Scott and Plasma are squared off.

Plasma "chambers" his leg preparing to throw a side kick.

Scott defends by stepping back and catching the foot of Plasma with both hands.

With the leg secure, Scott tosses Plasma's leg to his right . . .

. . . bringing his opponent into range for a straight right.

Mixed martial arts is comprised of three main elements: striking, wrestling and submission. Wrestling is the segue way between the stand-up and the ground game. It's the clinch work that leads to a takedown, the double leg or ankle pick that takes the striker off his feet, and the big slam from a Greco Roman wrestler. Dan Severn was the first pure wrestler to step into the Octagon at UFC 4, and though it took him some time to understand striking and submission, it established the scoring component of "Octagon control."

Problem was, wrestlers were great at control — working top side of their opponents — but if they didn't know how to finish, it led to some fairly uneventful matches. Wrestlers flocked to MMA after the Olympics committee allowed the grapplers to compete for purse money outside the Games. They were strong, well-conditioned athletes with mental toughness who needed a home.

Amateur wrestlers, outside the Olympics, had no avenue for a spectator sport aside from MMA. Dan Gable and Cael Sanderson couldn't find elite avenues on pay-per-view or closed circuit TV like top-ranked boxers. So unless they wanted to try their hand at pro wrestling, MMA became a valid, post-college career to continue competing at the highest level.

Mark Schultz, the 1984 Olympic freestyle wrestling champion, showed up to corner a fighter at UFC 9 against Gary Goodridge. He had not wrestled in eight years, but had studied submission for four. On one night's notice, he took a fight and dominated Goodridge from start to finish. Mark Coleman, Randy Couture, Matt Lindland, Dan

Henderson, Kevin Randleman, Quinton Jackson, Tito Ortiz and Matt Hughes have all made their mark on the sport, utilizing their wrestling accolades to become MMA champions.

Now wrestlers are training specifically for a post-wrestling career in MMA at earlier ages. At any given school, the chance of a boxing or jiu-jitsu program is unlikely, but wrestling is a major amateur sport in many schools. It has become one of the most dominant foundations in MMA, arguably surpassing jiu-jitsu, because programs are so readily available. Wrestling produces fast-twitch muscle fibers that give them an edge over straight submission athletes, but over time, wrestlers have adjusted their games to compete against the modern day mixed martial artist.

Brock Lesnar is a 2000 NCAA heavyweight wrestling champion, who shot up the ranks of the UFC to become the UFC heavyweight champion. Shane Carwin is another collegiate wrestling champion; both men are fast, strong and powerful. Jon Jones is one of the UFC's rising stars, a light heavyweight state champion wrestler, who mixes up his amazing takedowns and throws with crazy, yet accurate punches and deadly elbows. Georges St. Pierre has been called one of the best MMA wrestlers, and yet, he has never even won a wrestling title. He has dispatched several collegiate wrestling champs including Jon Fitch, Josh Kosheck and Matt Hughes.

In the wrestling section, MMA Worldwide is proud to present techniques from Greco Roman wrestler Randy Couture, catch wrestler Erik Paulson, sambo stylist Fedor Emelianenko, freestyle wrestling champion Vladimir Matyushenko and Olympic silver medalist Matt Lindland. These techniques cover a wide range of movements, including the clinch, takedowns, throws, escapes, top side control and positioning.

See intro on page 14.

Clinch Defense...

Pat Miletich is clinched by opponent Matt Hughes.

Miletich steps between Hughes' legs with his left foot, pushes his hips forward, and then straightens his back so Hughes can't pull him down.

Miletich then locks his hands around Hughes' waist and pulls him inward.

Pat then steps behind him with his right foot while keeping his hands locked, and prepares to trip Hughes down.

SEE PAGE 176 FOR AN EXCLUSIVE MMA WORLDWIDE PACKAGE DEAL!

See intro on page 43.

Takedown Defense

Jackson's opponent shoots in for the takedown.

Jackson sprawls by kicking his legs backwards, so his opponent can't reach him. Jackson's chest lands on his opponent's back, forcing his face towards the ground.

Jackson puts his left forearm against his opponent's jaw. He then locks his hands behind his opponent's left arm.

From here Jackson can use knees to to strike his opponent's head to finish the fight.

BAM!

John is one of five brothers of the world-renowned Machado Brazilian Jiu-Jitsu martial art family. Born in Rio De Janeiro, Brazil: John began his jiu-jitsu training over twenty years ago. Dominating the competitive arena of Brazilian Jiu-Jitsu in his native country, seizing every major title and competitive award from 1982-1990, John holds the prestigious rank of 4th degree black belt in Brazilian Jiu-Jitsu.

Dominating the Brazilian Jiu-Jitsu scene both in the U.S. and in international competition, John is one of the most admired and respected Brazilian Jiu-Jitsu practitioners in the world today. Recognized and respected for his outstanding fighting and competitive accomplishments, as well as his teaching expertise, John is in demand throughout the world as one of the foremost authorities in the martial arts. John's talent has been showcased in several major motion pictures and television appearances. *For more info on John, visit www.johnmachado.net.*

Defense to Single Leg

1 John is standing over his opponent, who has open guard. John steps in between his opponent's legs with his right leg. He uses his hands to control his opponent's legs.

2 John's opponent sits up and grabs John's right leg with his left arm, to go for the single leg takedown.

3 John swings his left leg backwards towards his opponent's left side.

4 Now John sits back and traps his opponent's left leg with his left arm. Notice how John holds his opponent's head up with his right arm for control.

5 John continues to roll back bringing his opponent flat on his back. He also continues to pull his opponent's left leg up.

6 Here you can see how John pulls the left leg up for the knee bar.

7 John locks his hands around his opponent's left leg. His right foot hooks under his opponent's right leg and he arches his hips and applies pressure to the knee bar.

Defense to Single Leg (Options 2 & 3)

From this position (page 49, photo 5) John's opponent kicks his left leg straight down to avoid the knee bar. John now has the option of going to side mount.

John kicks his opponent's left leg straight down with his own left leg.

Now John brings his right leg straight up and over his opponent's left leg.

Here you can see how John brings his right leg out.

Now John rolls on top of his opponent and secures the side mount.

From this position John also has the option of going to full mount.

John pulls his right leg out as before.

Except this time, John swings his left leg over his opponent's body for the full mount.

This is where John ends up.

Bob Anderson has been a fixture in MMA as one of the most recognizable wrestling coaches in the industry. Having coached some of MMA's best since they were children, like Dan Henderson and Randy Couture, Anderson has been able to turn his great wrestling coaching abilities into MMA specific wrestling techniques as well.

Reversal To Double Leg Takedown

Bob Anderson is faced off with Bryon Schnell.

Bryon shoots in for a double leg takedown.

Bob does not have time to sprawl so Bryon gets the takedown. Bob immediately moves his hips out to the side. In this case the left side because of where Bryon's head is.

As soon as Bob hits the mat he forces Bryon's head down with his left hand and braces himself with his right hand. Here you can see how Bob has scooted his hips out to the left.

Now, Bob kicks his left leg over Bryon's body for the sweep.

After the sweep Bob lands in the mounted position.

With his right hand Bob pulls Bryon's head straight up and he steps up with his right leg.

Bob wraps his right leg around Bryon's neck.

Now, Bob locks his right foot behind his left knee. Bob forces Bryon's right arm across his neck and drops his weight for the choke. Bob can also strike from this position.

Takedown Defense to Roll

Bob is squared off with his son, Dru.

Dru shoots in for the takedown.

Bob immediately steps back with his right foot so Dru cannot get the double leg. Bob can also control Dru's hands with his right hand and try to break the takedown.

Dru gets a good lock on Bob's leg so Bob must go to his next option. Bob uses a butt drag to pull Dru towards him and pushes Dru's head down with his right hand.

Bob steps forward with his right leg and traps Dru's head between his legs.

With his right hand, Bob reaches through Dru's legs and grabs inside his left thigh.

Now Bob sits backwards and rolls Dru over.

Here is where Dru ends up after the roll. Bob immediately starts to roll on top of Dru for side control. Notice how Bob continues to control Dru's left leg with his right hand.

Bob ends up in side mount.

Takedown Defense to Inside Leg Trip

Bob is squared off with Dru.

As Dru shoots in for the takedown Bob immediately steps back with his right leg. This forces Dru to take the single leg.

Bob uses a butt drag with his left hand to pull Dru towards him and forces Dru's head down with his right hand.

Bob pushes forward off his right foot and steps between Dru's legs with his left foot, hooking Dru's right leg for the inside ankle trip.

Bob bumps his hips forward to knock Dru backwards.

Dru lands on his back. Bob controls his right leg with his left hand.

Bob throws Dru's right leg to the side and steps in to gain side control.

Bob pins Dru's right arm to the mat with his left leg.

Then Bob goes to knee-on-belly position with his right leg. Notice how Bob controls Dru's head with his left hand so Dru cannot bridge. From here Bob can finish the fight with punches.

There are very few combat athletes in the world who can be recognized solely by their nickname. But when anyone in mixed martial arts around the world hears the name "The Westside Strangler," there is no doubt it is Chris Brennan. A unique breed of athlete, Brennan is a master grappler, no-holds-barred star, and elite submission fighter who not only talks the talk but also walks the walk. Since beginning in Brazilian jiu-jitsu in the early '90s, Brennan has continually honed both his teaching and fighting skills to become an acknowledged master of both. One of the few combat athletes to have competed successfully in UFC, Pride, KOTC, Gladiator Challenge, Extreme Challenge and more, Brennan recently added another feather to his cap when he had the extreme honor of being the first grappler to be given an open invitation to the 2005 ADCC World Submission Wrestling Championships. "Only the best of the best get invited to compete in the ADCC tournament," says Brennan. "So to get that call to compete was a validation of all the time, effort and passion I've put into the sport over the years."

For information on grappling classes at Chris Brennan's Next Generation Fighting Academy, or to inquire about NHB fight training or Chris' worldwide seminar tour, visit http://chrisbrennan.com

High Crotch to Double-Leg Takedown

Chris Brennan is tied up with his brother Jake, with his left hand on Jake's neck and right hand on Jake's left elbow.

Chris releases Jake's neck, shoots for the takedown, and grabs Jake's left leg with his left arm. Notice how Chris uses his right arm to bring Jake's left arm over his head. If he were to let Jake get an underhook he would be thrown to his back.

Chris wraps his right arm around Jake's leg.

Bringing his left arm across, Chris grabs Jake's right leg for a double-leg.

Chris brings his right foot forward and posts it on the ground.

Arching his back, Chris lifts Jake off the ground.

Chris dumps Jake on his back and ends up in side mount. Notice how Chris controls Jake's legs to avoid being put into Jake's guard.

Erik Paulson is a former two-time world Shooto champion who was the first American to win a Shooto title in Japan. Defending the title for 9 years, Erik became the first superstar of the Shooto world. He now travels the world giving Shooto, grappling, and martial arts seminars and recently opened a new school, Orange County Shootwrestling, in southern California. Here he shows a few of his favorite techniques.

For more information on seminars or classes with Erik Paulson, or on his complete line of training DVDs, visit www.erikpaulson.com.

Fighting Off A Wall

Erik is squared off with "Big Dave" with his back to the wall.

Dave throws a jab, which Erik blocks with his right hand.

Dave rushes in to tie up with Erik and force him against the wall. Dave gets an overhook with his right arm and an underhook with his left arm.

Erik immediately works for proper head position as shown here. He also pushes Dave's left arm back with his right hand.

Now that Erik has created some space, he can reach up for the Thai clinch.

To avoid the clinch, Dave pushes into Erik. Erik immediately brings his right hand down and hooks Dave's left arm.

Now, Erik steps out to his right and pushes Dave into the wall.

Erik quickly loads a right hand…

...and finishes with a straight right to Dave's jaw.

Double Leg Defense Against A Wall

Erik is pinned up against the wall. Dave drops to a double leg to take Erik down.

Erik grabs both of Dave's arms on the triceps. Erik pushes his hips forward and pulls Dave's arms straight up.

Now, Erik reaches down and gets an underhook with his left arm.

Then he gets an underhook with his right arm.

Now, Erik starts to step out to this right.

In one, powerful motion, Erik steps behind Dave and throws Dave's left arm over his head so he can come out the back door. Notice how Erik's right leg is up high. He can bump Dave's hips forward with this leg to help the move.

Erik ends up behind Dave.

Erik pushes Dave into the wall.

Dave turns to face Erik, who is already set to strike.

Erik finishes with a right hand to the jaw.

RJ Clifford and Joey Bareng are both alumni of the San Francisco State Wrestling team. Joey was a Rocky Mountain Athletic Conference Champion in 2003 as well as a NCAA Division II All-American in 2004, and assistant coach for San Francisco for the 2004-05 and 2005-06 seasons. RJ was a Junior College All-American in 2002 before wrestling for San Francisco as well as a BJJ blue belt under Pallo "Junior" Gazze. Both are using their seasoned wrestling experience as a base for their MMA debuts they are currently training for. Look for them in the cage this summer. To book RJ or Joey for seminars, contact RJ at urge152@yahoo.com. For personal training, contact Joey at camogator@yahoo.com.

Breaking the Clinch to the Claw (Throw)

Joey has RJ in the clinch.

RJ reaches up and grabs Joey's neck with his right hand.

With his left hand, RJ reaches under Joey's right arm and grabs his own right arm.

Here you can see how RJ grabs his right bicep.

Now, RJ steps outside Joey's right leg.

RJ lifts his left elbow to shuck Joey's arm off of his neck and break the clinch.

Once Joey's arm goes by, RJ immediately reaches through Joey's legs with his left arm.

Notice how RJ still has control of Joey's neck with his right hand.

RJ lifts Joey up for the slam...

...and drops him onto his back. Notice how RJ stays chest to chest with Joey.

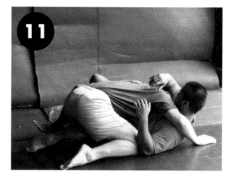

RJ ends up with side mount on Joey.

SEE PAGE 176 FOR AN EXCLUSIVE MMA WORLDWIDE PACKAGE DEAL!

Breaking the Clinch to a Throw - Option 2

From this position, RJ has another option.

Notice how RJ still has control of Joey's neck with his right arm.

Joey turns toward RJ to try and regain his position. RJ keeps his head tight against Joey's arm to keep it from slipping through. RJ also gets a tighter wrap on Joey's neck with his right arm.

As soon as RJ wraps his arm around Joey's neck he grabs his left bicep.

Here you can see how RJ locks the arm triangle.

Now, RJ steps his right leg behind Joey's right leg to go for the throw.

RJ turns his torso and throws Joey over his hips.

Here is where they end up after the throw. Notice how RJ still has the lock on Joey's neck.

Now, RJ kicks his right leg through to get into a sitting position. He leans back, pulling Joey's head up, finishing the choke / neck crank.

Clark "The Irish Bulldog" Bevans is an accomplished wrestler with 25 years experience, 21 of which on the national level and 18 at the international level. After a very decorated high school career, Clark wrestled for the United States Marine Corps under Major Dan Hicks and legends Steve Fraser and Bill Martell. Known for his very aggressive fighting style and "big air" takedowns Clark has ten amateur fights and is undefeated as a professional with a 4 - 0 record coming off his most recent victory, a TKO in 1:04.

Clark also owns three Gold's Gyms and is currently remodeling his Huntington Beach gym to include a fighting studio. For more information please e-mail him at crbevans@hotmail.com.

High Crotch Takedown

Junior and Clark are squared off.

Clark lowers his level under Junior's jab.

Clark takes a short step in and shoots a high crotch on Junior's left leg. Once the leg is secure Clark steps around bringing his hips in close.

Clark then steps around behind Junior and locks his hands around Junior's waist.

Clark places his right knee to the outside of Junior's right knee and pivots Junior's body to the right. . .

. . . bringing Junior down.

Clark finishes with strikes.

Countering a Muay Thai Clinch With a Take Down

1 Junior has a Thai clinch on Clark.

2 With his left hand, Clark lifts Junior's right arm over his head and then shoots in for the takedown. Notice how Clark grabs inside Junior's right leg with his right hand.

3 Clark steps around, bringing his hips in close and locks his hands together.

4 Using his legs for power, Clark lifts Junior straight up.

5 Now, Clark spins around and drops Junior on his back.

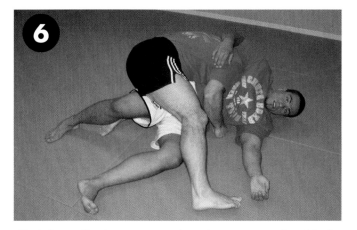

6 Clark immediately steps over into the mount as they hit the ground.

7 From here, Clark can finish with strikes.

Mac Danzig is the current King of the Cage and Gladiator Challenge World Champion at 155 lbs. Mac recently gained a great deal of recognition for his win over Takumi Nakayama at King of the Cage's "Execution Day". Many call Danzig's performance the best of any lightweight all year long, but Mac still hasn't reached the level he desires. Mac says he has plans of defending his title a few times and then he would like to travel to Japan for Bushido. Mac trains under Romie Aram at Millennia Jiu-Jitsu. For more info on training with Mac and his teammates visit www.millenniajiujitsu.com.

Takedown from the Tie-up

Mac Danzig is tied up with John Alessio. Mac has an under hook with his right arm and his left hand is against John's right bicep.

Mac steps back and brings his head inside for dominant head position.

Mac grabs John's neck with his left hand. Now, he pulls John down with both hands. Notice that Mac drops down and uses his weight to help pull John down.

Mac raises his body above John's head and locks his left arm around John's neck.

Now, Mac shoots his right arm across John's back, towards John's right hip.

Mac twists his body to throw John to the mat. Mac forces John's head down with his left arm and throws with his right arm.

Mac ends up with side mount on John. From here, Mac can go for the neck crank.

UFC veteran and former IFL coach, Matt Lindland is one of the most decorated wrestlers ever to enter MMA. A silver medalist at the 2000 Olympic Games in Greco-Roman wrestling, he has dazzled fans with his takedowns and slippery ground work. As one of the founding members of Team Quest in Gresham, Oregon, Matt was kind enough to take time out of his busy schedule to show us some of the moves that have carried his career.

Single Leg Finish Against the Cage

Joker has Matt up against the wall or cage in an over-under clinch. This move could also work in the open mat away from the wall.

Joker drops down for a single leg.

Matt defends the single by locking in a kimura on Joker's left arm.

Joker then releases the single leg and snakes his right hand down to Matt's calf.

Joker then drops to his hip maintaining his hold on Matt's left leg.

Joker then uses the hold to role Matt to his back and off the wall.

Joker then turns into Matt...

...ending up in side mount.

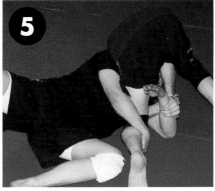

Then celebrates his takedown!

At seven years old PJ Scharf is one of the top wrestlers in the nation in his division. Wrestling since the age of three, PJ has accomplished more in wrestling in his seven years alive than most will in a lifetime. On top of countless medals, trophies, and awards, PJ has over 200 wins in competition. His aggressive style and work ethic have put PJ's skills a head higher than the rest of his division. PJ took time away from his Legos to show Tapout Magazine some of his favorite moves.

Duck Under

PJ (on right) and Parter are squared off.

PJ ties up with Parter using a collar tie with his right hand on Parter's neck (palm down) and grips Parter's right arm with his left hand.

PJ gets Parter to step into him by taking a circle step to his right and pulling Parter into him.

PJ drops his level and takes a deep step with his right foot while pulling Parter's right arm over his head. Notice how PJ keeps his head tight against Parter's side.

PJ then circles and steps behind Parter while wrapping his left arm around Parter's waist. PJ maintains a firm grip with his right arm on the collar tie.

PJ then finishes the takedown by pulling down on the collar tie.

Sweep Single

PJ and Parter are squared off.

PJ takes a step to the right, creating an angle on Parter.

PJ then drops his level and shoots on Parter's left leg. PJ grips Parter's knee with his right arm, drops his knee just outside of Parter's foot, and posts on the ground with his left hand.

PJ then sweeps behind Parter dropping to both knees and gripping Parter's ankle with his left hand. Notice how PJ keeps his head tight against Parter's side the whole time.

Here is another look at his position.

PJ then drops his head lower on his opponent's leg and switches his right hand off Parter's left leg and onto Parter's right ankle.

PJ then drives his shoulder into Parter while pulling on both legs forcing Parter to the ground. PJ then climbs on top securing the takedown.

Elbow Pop Double Leg

Parter has his hands posted on PJ's shoulders.

PJ moves his hands (palms up) under Parter's elbows.

PJ then pops Parter's elbows up, drops his level, and steps in deep with his right foot all at the same time.

PJ then grips both his hands around Parter's legs and behind his knees keeping his elbows in tight. PJ also brings his left leg around and plants his foot to his left while keeping his hips under him.

PJ then lifts up Parter by sliding his body around Parter's right side and bringing his hips tight against Parter's.

PJ then lifts Parter's hips over his shoulder...

...and finishes the slam in side mount.

Snap Down to Neck Crank

PJ and Parter are tied up. PJ has a collar tie.

PJ snaps Parter's head down while sprawling his own hips out bringing Parter down to the mat. PJ then wraps his left arm in an over hook maintaining control.

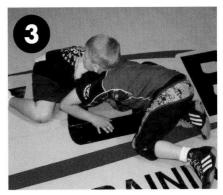

PJ then takes his left arm and gets a deep under hook placing his left palm on Parter's back.

From the view on the opposite side you can see PJ wrapping his right arm around Parter's neck...

...and cupping his chin.

PJ then drives his left hand across the back driving Parter's shoulders to the mat. Notice how PJ uses his legs to drive Parter down.

PJ then starts to slide his hips into Parter

PJ slides his left leg under his right bringing his side to the mat. At the same time PJ is pulling up on Parter's head finishing the neck crank.

Needing no introduction, Randy "The Natural" Couture has been a mainstay in the UFC both at light heavyweight and heavyweight. The first man to win titles in two separate weight classes, Couture has become a superstar and ambassador for the sport of MMA. His Greco-Roman wrestling credentials have given Couture an effective fighting style of clinch work and dirty boxing that wears down an opponent to the point of giving up.

From Randy Couture's Victory Belt Book, Wrestling for Fighting: The Natural Way, available at www.victorybelt.com and bookstores everywhere.

Arm Throw

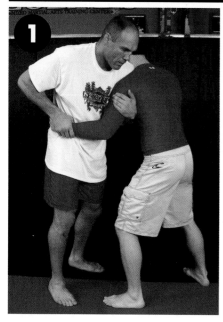

Randy has Glen in an arm-drag position with his right hand on Glen's left wrist and his left hand cuffed around the back of his left arm.

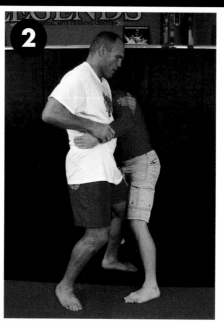

Randy steps his left leg between Glen's legs, kicks his hips forward and pulls Glen's left arm into him forcing Glen off balance. Glen must now step his right foot out to maintain balance.

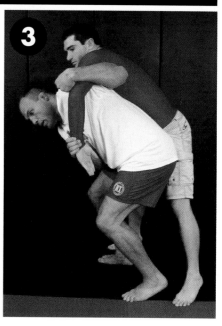

Randy then pivots stepping his right leg in between Glen's legs. Notice Randy has dropped his levels positioning his hips under Glen's.

Randy then corkscrews his hips and pulls Glen's left arm over his left shoulder. Randy leans forward and drops his weight as if he were doing a forward roll.

Glen slams to the mat. From here Randy will turn into him and establish top control.

Counter to a Body Lock

1

Joker has Randy in a body lock.

2

Randy brings his right leg tight against the outside of Joker's left leg.

3

Randy then brings his right arm around Joker's head and tight against his ear.

4

Randy then pushes in with his knee and pulls Joker's head down and out, getting Joker off-balance.

5

Randy then uses the space created to under hook with his left arm.

6

Randy then hikes up the under hook creating space...

7

...for a right knee to the body.

Counter to a Thai Clinch

Freddy has Randy in a Thai clinch.

Randy comes around Freddy's head with his left arm and cups across his ear. He grips Freddy's waist with his right hand.

Randy then pulls with his left arm while pushing forward with his left shoulder breaking the clinch. He also pulls in with his right arm.

Here is a closer look at the position.

Randy slides his right arm up from the waist and into an under hook.

Randy then cranks up on the under hook and turns Freddy's hips out.

Randy then steps across with his left foot, drops his level, and prepares to knee tap Freddy.

Randy drives Freddy to the mat by pushing with his under hook and pulling at the knee.

Then quickly gains side mount.

Antonio Rodrigo Nogueira is one of the best Brazilian jiu-jitsu artists in MMA. A successful career in PrideFC saw the heavyweight submit the likes of Mark Coleman, Dan Henderson and Mirko "Cro Cop" Filipovic as well as earn the heavyweight belt. When Zuufa, the parent company of the UFC, purchased PrideFC, Nogueira came over to the US and won the UFC heavyweight title as well to go along with his former PrdieFC belt.

Side Mount to Arm Bar

Nogueira has Freddy side mounted.

Nogueira strikes from the top, causing Freddy to bring his arm back in defense.

Nogueira lifts his hips off the mat with his left leg and right arm.

He then steps over Freddy's head with his right leg.

Nogueira isolates Freddy's right arm.

He then brings his left leg over Freddy.

Nogueira brings his knees together and drops off to the side.

Nogueira extends his hips and finishes the submission.

Dean "The Boogie Man" Lister is one of the most well respected submission fighters in the world. An absolute division champion in the prestigious Abu Dhabi Championships and a US National Sambo Champion, Lister's grappling credentials are some of the best in the world. Lister is also a seasoned MMA fighter having fought some of the world's best in both PrideFC and the UFC with a professional record of 11 – 7. For more, log on to www.deanlister.com or you can train with Dean at his new gym Xtreme Couture San Diego.

Hip Throw Setup

Dean has an under hook with his right arm and is controlling his opponent's right wrist with his left hand.

Stepping behind his opponent with his right leg, Dean fakes a drag back.

His opponent counters by stepping his left leg out from behind Dean's leg.

As soon as his opponent attempts to counter, Dean steps across his opponent's hips.

Dean then turns his hips into his opponent.

With his hips in Dean can now execute the throw by pushing his hips in and elevating his opponent.

Dean controls his opponent's fall so he can...

...establish control on top.

Roll Through Single Leg Finish

Dean has his opponent's left leg in a single leg attack.

Dean releases his grip and threads his right arm through his opponent's legs blocking his far thigh. His left hand remains on his opponent's left leg.

Maintaining his grip on his opponent's right thigh and left knee, Dean rolls to his back behind his opponent.

Dean then sucks his opponent back over his body...

...bringing his opponent to his back.

Dean can now pass to side mount.

Inside Leg Trip

Dean and his opponent are tied up in an over under or 50/50 position.

Dean points to his opponent's leg opposite his opponent's head so he can not see the trip coming.

Sagging his hips down, Dean threads his left leg through his opponent's legs and wraps around the back of his right leg.

Dean then drops to his knee driving forward...

...bringing his opponent to the ground.

Born in Africa, Sokoudjou was discovered by none other than Pride champion Dan Henderson and the rest of the Team Quest family in Temecula, California. Sokoudjou started out with Olympic hopes in judo but soon found a passion for MMA. In is Pride debut he knocked out top five light heavyweight Antonio Rogerio Nogueira. In his second Pride match he knocked out another top five light heavyweight in Ricardo Arona.

Takedown Counter to a Body Kick

Sokoudjou and Ryan are squared off.

Ryan throws a body kick that Sokoudjou catches.

Sokoudjou then uses his free hand and brings it behind the back of Ryan's neck.

He then steps through with his right leg behind Ryan's standing leg...

...to trip him. Notice Sokoudjou is rotating because he is using his hold on Ryan's neck to swing Ryan down.

Sokoudjou remains standing and maintains the hold on Ryan's leg...

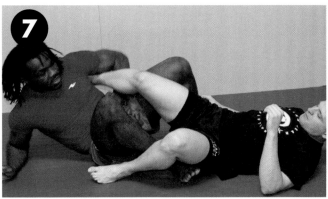

...so he can fall back into a leg lock.

Greg Nelson is the head instructor and owner of Minnesota Martial Arts Academy who boasts a stable of fighters including Sean Sherk, Brock Lesnar, Nick Thompson, Dave Menne and many others. An accomplished wrestler at the University of Minnesota, a certified Muay Thai instructor and Brazilian jiu-jitsu black belt, Nelson can do it all. Perhaps no school teaches better setups, positioning and takedowns against the fence than Minnesota Martial Arts Academy.

Double Leg Takedown in the Corner

Greg is attempting a double leg take-down in the corner of the cage. His hips are low, his shoulders are tight against RJ's waist and his arms are wrapped around his legs.

Because RJ's weight is on his back foot, Greg grips around the top of the back of RJ's knee and pulls in bending his leg.

Now Greg can pull RJ's legs into him.

Keeping his shoulders tight, Greg pulls RJ's legs in between his legs driving RJ to the mat.

Maintaining control and pinching RJ's knees together, Greg elevates RJ's legs . . .

. . . so he can slide his hips over the top into the mount.

Slam Takedown Against Cage

1 Greg is attempting a double leg take-down in the corner of the cage.

2 Locking his hands around the back of RJ, Greg steps in with his legs keeping his hips low.

3 With everything in position Greg can now lift RJ.

4 Here Greg takes a step back. He could also walk to his own corner where he can hear his coaches better.

5 Now with space to slam Greg can drive RJ down to the mat.

6 Once down Greg maintains his grip and shoulder pressure. Notice RJ's left leg is in between Greg's legs.

7 To pass, Greg blocks RJ's left leg with his right arm and elevates his own left leg.

8 Now Greg can clear his leg and land in side mount.

9 Greg blocks RJ's right bicep, moves to knee on belly position and strikes.

Under Hook Takedown Against the Cage

1

RJ has his back against the flat area of the cage with Greg squared off against him.

2

Greg throws a jab . . .

3

. . . a right straight . . .

4

. . . then pushes RJ against the cage.

5

Greg immediately ties up RJ in the clinch. He has a high under hook with his right arm, controlling RJ's bicep with his left hand and has his right knee in tight between RJ's legs.

6

Greg cranks his under hook up higher while lifting RJ's left leg with his right leg.

7

Here is a close up of their feet.

8

Continuing to drive with the under hook Greg elevates RJ's leg with his right foot and reaches for his other leg.

9

Once Greg has driven RJ's hips to the mat . . .

10

. . . he slides his right shin against across RJ's right thigh. Notice Greg's left foot is still posted out maintaining pressure.

11

To set up an elbow strike, Greg grabs RJ's wrist and extends it outward.

12

He then quickly slides it off and into RJ's face.

Double Leg Take Down Against the Cage

Greg is going for a double leg take down on RJ who is against the cage.

RJ spreads his legs out for balance so Greg drives his right knee against the back of RJ's knee.

Greg squeezes RJ's right knee in so he can grab around the back of RJ's knees.

Now Greg can pull RJ's legs out from under him.

Once RJ's hips hit the mat Greg still keeps his shoulders pressed against RJ's torso keeping RJ from sliding up the cage.

Greg uses his left foot and right knee to trap RJ's thighs together.

Now he reaches for RJ's right wrist and extends it outward . . .

. . . so he can bring his left knee on it and trap it so he can strike to RJ's head.

See bio on page 54.

Single Leg to Inside Trip

Fedor has a right collar tie and a left tricep grip. His opponent has the same grip.

In order to penetrate in for the takedown, Fedor ducks his head underneath his opponent's right collar tie. To begin this process, he grips his opponent's right elbow with his left hand.

As Fedor forces his opponent's right arm upward using his grip on his elbow, he drops his elevation and ducks his head underneath his opponent's right arm.

Continuing to drop his elevation, Fedor hooks his left hand around the back of his opponent's right knee and begins pulling upward on his leg.

Fedor straightens his posture and draws his opponent's right leg into Fedor's body using his left hand.

Now he twists his body in a counterclockwise direction and uses his right collar tie to push his opponent's upper body toward his right side. As he does this, Fedor steps his right leg to the inside of his opponent's left leg and thrusts his hips forward.

As his opponent lands hard on his back, Fedor remains standing. Fedor is now in a perfect position to attack one of his legs with a submission, pass his guard, or unleash with ground and pound.

To purchase books, go to www.victorybelt.com

Outside Trip (From Over-Under Control)

Fedor is tied up with his opponent in the over-under position. Fedor pushes his butt backward, drives his shoulders into his opponent's shoulders, and grips his hands together just above his waistline.

Fedor sucks his arms toward his body, forcing his opponent to posture. At the same time, he circles his left leg around his opponent's right leg and plants his foot behind his right heel.

Continuing to circle around his opponent, Fedor sits toward the mat and begins pulling his opponent backward over his left leg.

As Fedor pulls his opponent over his left leg, he twists his body hard in a counterclockwise direction.

Fedor continues to twist his body in a counter-clockwise direction and pulls his opponent over his left leg.

Still twisting his body in a counterclockwise direction, Fedor forces his opponent onto his left side the instant he lands on his back. Now Fedor wraps his right arm around the left side of his opponent's head, posts on his left foot, and begins sliding his right leg underneath his left leg.

Fedor slides his right leg underneath his opponent's right arm, grips around the back of his opponent's neck and settles his hips. Now Fedor can strike or work for a submission.

with **Vladimir Matyushenko**

Vladimir "The Janitor" Matyushenko was a successful international wrestler for Belarus before moving to the United States and taking up MMA as a profession. Sporting a 24-4 record, Matyushenko has fought in the UFC, Affliction and went unde-feated in the IFL as their only light heavyweight champion. His takedowns and control are nearly unparalleled in MMA.

To learn more about "The Janitor" or his gym in El Segundo, CA, log on to www.vladthejanitor.com.

Shot Defense to Takedown

Steve and Vladimir are squared off.

Steve attempts a single leg takedown so Vladimir defends by pulling his leg away and pushing on Steve's head redi-recting him away from his leg.

Vladimir keeps his hands on the back of Steve's head and throws a left knee to his face.

Keeping the pressure on Steve's head, Vladimir uses the strike to keep Steve dazed so . . .

. . . he can shoot in for a double leg takedown.

Vladimir lifts Steve onto his shoulders.

He then rotates Steve's legs out to the side . . .

. . . to avoid Steve's guard and land in side mount.

Bodylock to Mount

Vladimir starts by pummeling Steve's left hand by palming the inside of his wrist and swimming it out.

He repeats with Steve's left hand clearing Steve's arms to the outside and putting his arms inside.

Vladimir then steps in deep with his hips and gets a body lock on Steve. Vladimir has his right arm under Steve's left arm and his left arm over Steve's right arm.

Pulling Steve tight, Vladimir gets Steve's hips in tight to his hips.

Now Vladimir can step his left knee behind Steve's right knee and crank Steve to the mat.

As Steve is falling to the mat, Vladimir makes sure to step over Steve with his right leg . . .

. . . landing in the mount.

Here Vladimir can strike successfully.

Brandon Slay is the 2000 Olympic Gold medalist. To do this Slay defeated reigning Olympic champion Saitiev in the 2nd round, ending a 5 year un-beaten run for the now 3 time Russian Olympic champion. Slay is a graduate of the prestigious Wharton School of Business. He enjoys "giving back" by teaching kids through an organization he founded called Greater Gold. Slay has taught several classes at Memphis Judo & Jiu-Jitsu, and is a natural to submission wrestling. For more info: (www.BrandonSlay.com)

PHOTOGRAPHER: Mindy Busy, 3-Cubed Photography (www.3-cubed.com)

Double Leg Takedown

Slay gets Jeff to reach up with his "I reach you reach" setup.

Slay lowers his level, with his legs coiled like a spring.

Slay springs up (like a plane taking off not downwards like landing the plane) at a 45% angle. Notice Slay's shoulder hits Jeff hard before his knee briefly hits the mat.

Knee hits only for an instant. Slay uses his hands to chop at Jeff's knees, then he pulls his arms back like a "lat row".

Slay brings his trail leg up at a 90% angle for power, while using his head to push sideways.

Slay pivots his right foot like a wind-shield wiper to get to a perpendicular angle.

Slay quickly steps his right foot up and sideways, pressuring sideways into Jeff (the direction Jeff's head is pointing). It is a common mistake to drive forward into the guy thus landing in his guard or a guillotine.

This motion of Slay taking several steps sideways while chopping Jeff's knees and driving with his head will sweep Jeff's legs out to the side.

As Slay runs Jeff down, just before hitting the mat, he reaches inside with his left hand to pull Jeff's left leg up, making it difficult for Jeff to jump guard or even get the 1/2 guard.

Double Leg - Defense

Jeff is in deep on a double leg (ready to step across and finish).

On the way down, Slay reaches his left arm over Jeff's back and his right hand on Jeff's knee.

Slay uses Jeff's momentum while Jeff is "running him down".

As Slay goes down to the mat, he pulls Jeff in and lifts his left leg to keep from being mounted.

Slay quickly brings his knees in tight, ready to pop his hips up as he bridges & rolls.

Slay keeps Jeff's momentum going, rolling Jeff through.

Slay throws Jeff by, preventing the takedown, so both scramble in a neutral position.

Slide By

Slay and Jeff both have an over & under position.

Slay pushes his weight into Jeff, ready to hit the slide by, he pushes down to loosen Jeff's underhook.

As Slay feels Jeff pushing back, Slay lowers his level & steps to the side.

Notice how Jeff's weight goes forward almost over Slay's back.

Slay finds himself in his favorite position - Double Leg finish, ready to chop Jeff's knees.

Slay steps across sideways, lifting with his left hand & chopping with his right arm, using his head to drive Jeff to Slay's right.

As Jeff is on his way down, Slay reaches inside with his left hand to sweep Jeff's right knee out.

Shown from the other angle, Slay switches hands to prevent Jeff from getting full or 1/2 guard.

Slay continues pressuring into Jeff while stepping sideways, lifting Jeff's left knee.

Slay scores a takedown and finishes in side control.

Snap down to a Choke

Slay has just pressured into Jeff to get Jeff to push back.

As Jeff is pushing back, Slay snaps Jeff's head down and pulls him down on his wrist.

To keep Jeff's head down, Slay slams his shoulder & chest on Jeff's upper back, notice Slay's hand positioning.

Slay lowers his level which brings his weight down on Jeff's head.

Slay quickly sinks his arm deeper, wrapping his hand tight on top of Jeff's neck, elbow pointing down.

Slay grabs Jeff's elbow and lifts it up & back towards his hip.

Slay sinks his right hand deeper to Jeff's shoulder to tighten everything up.

To finish the submission, Slay arches his chest into Jeff while pulling both his elbows back.

Born on a US military base in Yokouska, Japan, the Filipino fighter Mark Munoz is another big up and comer on the UFC roster. After a high school wrestling career highlighted by two state championships, Munoz was recruited to NCAA powerhouse Oklahoma State by wrestling legend John Smith. As a four year starter, Munoz compiled 121 wins, sixth on the all-time winning list of the Cowboy wrestling dynasty. He captured two Big 12 titles including the outstanding wrestler honor of the conference in his senior year and earned back-to-back All-American honors at 197 pounds, capping off with a NCAA title as a senior in 2001. Encouraged by his friend and fellow coaching partner at UC Davis Urijah Faber, Munoz began training in MMA and made his pro debut in 2007 and has since racked up a record of 8-1.

For more on Mark Munoz, log on to www.markmunoz.net.

Single Leg to Barzagar

Mark is squared off with his opponent. His opponent is in a south paw stance.

Mark steps in with a jab to his opponent's head. Notice how Mark steps to the outside of his opponent's foot and is blocking with his right hand.

Mark crouches down to begin his single leg shot.

Mark grabs the right leg of his opponent and presses his head firmly into his chest.

Mark steps forward with his right leg.

Mark moves to grab his opponent's other leg while still holding onto to the right leg.

Mark steps forward with his left leg and pushes off it while raising the opponent's right leg into the air and driving forward for the takedown.

Mark moves to side control by keeping his head pined against his opponent's chest while quickly transitioning his body so that it is perpendicular with the opponent's.

Mark secures side control by under-hooking his opponent's left shoulder with his right arm while keeping the opponent's right armpit sucked into Mark's hips, all while keeping downward pressure on his opponent.

50/50 Clinch to Foot Sweep

Mark is clinched with his opponent in a traditional stance with his right arm under-hooking his opponent's left.

Mark pulls with his under hook rotating his opponent 90 degrees and getting him off balance.

Mark fully turns his opponent around creating space between their hips. Notice Mark keeps his left hand on his opponent's right hip.

Another view of the same position from the previous photo.

Mark pulls his opponent's hips into his while beginning to lean backwards.

Mark rotates his upper body clockwise while tripping his opponent's left ankle initiating the takedown.

After taking down his opponent Mark establishes side control.

UFC middleweight Mark Muñoz brings a wealth of wrestling talent to the Octagon. As a four time member of the Big 12 Academic Squad, Muñoz was a two-time All-American for Oklahoma State finishing his collegiate career with a national championship in 2001. Muñoz's work ethic and skill set earned him an undefeated record of 5-0 prior to entering the UFC where he has since gone 3-1. Muñoz recently opened his own gym in Lake Forest, CA called the Reign Training Center.

For more on Mark Muñoz or his gym log on to www.markmunoz.net or www.train2reign.com.

Body Lock to Crank Down

Mark and Andre are in a 50/50 clinch. They each have an over hook and an under hook.

Mark drops his hips and lowers his arms around Andre's waist and locks in a body lock with an under hook with his right arm and Andre's right arm trapped under Mark's left arm.

Shrugging his right shoulder up, Mark steps to his right and gets to the side of Andre.

Now perpendicular to Andre, Mark brings his right knee behind Andre's knee.

From here, Mark can drag Andre over his knee and bring his back to the mat. . .

. . .and land in side control.

50/50 Clinch to Knee Tap

Mark and Andre are in a 50/50 clinch.

Mark drops his hips and goes for a body clinch.

With the body lock set, Mark attempts to step over Andre's left leg and drag him down for the takedown.

Andre counters the attempt by stepping his left foot back.

This sets up the knee tap because Andre's weight is now on his right foot. Mark drops his levels, pushes with his right arm and drops his left hand to Andre's right knee.

In this position all Mark has to do is drive his feet while pushing in with his right arm and pulling back with his left hand.

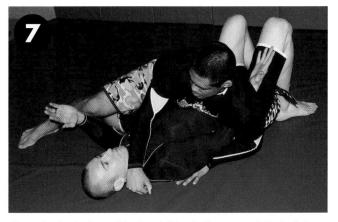

Once Andre is down Mark quickly circles around Andre's legs to avoid the guard and land in side mount.

Body Lock to Double Leg

Mark and Andre are in the 50/50 clinch.

Mark gets a body lock around Andre's waist.

In an attempt to drag Andre down, Mark steps his right foot over Andre's left foot.

Andre counters by stepping his left leg back.

Now that Andre's weight is falling forward, Mark drops his hips and wraps his arms around Andre's legs.

With Andre's body naturally wanting to fall forward, Mark turns the corner around Andre starts lifting Andre's legs up for the double leg.

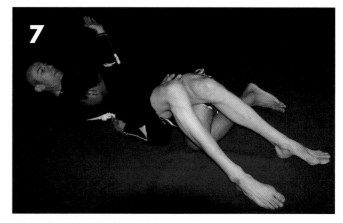

Throwing Andre's legs to the side means Mark lands in a side mount avoiding the guard.

50/50 Clinch to Inside Leg Trip

Mark and Andre are in a 50/50 clinch.

Mark pulls Andre's right side into him making him step with his right foot.

Once Andre's foot is planted Mark drops his hips and pushes into Andre while wrapping his left leg around Andre's right leg.

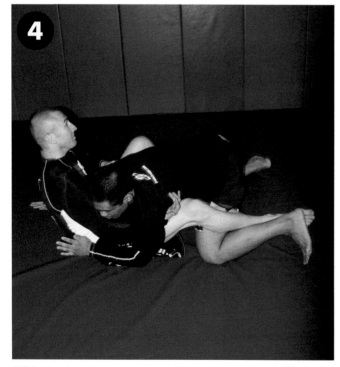

With the leg trapped, Mark continues pushing into Andre driving him into the mat. . .

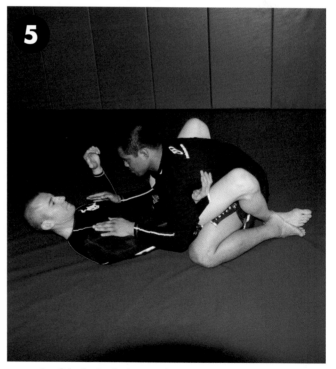

. . .and safely in Andre's guard.

Randy "The Natural" Couture is one of the most accomplished fighters in MMA history. Having won multiple UFC belts in both the light heavy and heavyweight divisions, he was the first to be champion at two different weight classes. A four time national champion in Greco-Roman wrestling, Couture's style of takedowns and ground and pound is the base for his MMA success. Here Randy shows us some of his takedowns that helped make him the champion he is today.

These techniques are from Randy's technique book Wrestling for Fighingt: The Natural Way by Victory Belt Publishing available at www.victorybelt.com or a book store near you.

Duck Under Off of an Underhook

Randy has an underhook with his left arm. Notice Randy has his underhook tight by gripping the top of Glen's right shoulder with his underhook hand. Randy has his forehead in tight to Glen's neck and is controlling Glen's left arm by gripping his bicep with his right hand.

Taking a short step forward with his left foot, Randy simultaneously pops Glen's right arm up with his left elbow, drops his hips slightly and pops his head under Glen's right arm.

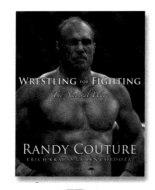

Randy now brings his left arm around Glen's waist and his right arm over Glen's left shoulder. While he is adjusting his hands, he turns his hips 90 degrees to his right and drives off his left foot pushing Glen off balance. From here Randy can simply drive Glen to the floor or go for a lift.

Counter Jab to Double-Leg

Randy is in his fighting stance, squared off with Glen.

Glen throws a left so Randy slips his punch by dipping his head slightly to the right side. To ensure that he doesn't redirect his punch, Randy uses his right hand to guide Glen's fist to the left side of Randy's head.

The instant Randy slips Glen's jab, he penetrates in for the double-leg by driving forward off his right foot, stepping his left foot between Glen's legs, and grabbing the back of his knees with both hands.

Randy blasts through Glen for the double-leg takedown by pushing off his right foot, taking an outward step with his left foot, and driving his head into the left side of Glen's body.

As Glen falls to the mat, Randy secures top position by pulling his legs in tight using both arms, dropping his left knee to the mat, and posting on his right foot driving his shoulders into Glen.

Slide Off by Over-Under Position

Randy is in the over-under position with Glen. They are chest to chest and each has an underhook with their left arms.

Randy attacks Glen's underhook with his right hand by gripping his elbow.

With that grip he pushes Glen's elbow out from under his arm pit and slides Glen's arm across his chest.

Pushing with his left foot, Randy lifts his underhook while pushing Glen's elbow with his right hand. This gets Glen off balance.

When Glen tries to readjust his position, Randy pushes Glen's left arm out from under his arm pit, pulls his own underhook out down to Glen's right knee and drops his hips in preparation for a double leg.

Randy now wraps his hands behind Glen's knees, drives his head in tight to Glen's side and posts on his right foot. From here Randy can lift Glen, drive him to the mat or spin behind him.

Mixed martial arts is comprised of three main elements: striking, wrestling and submission. Submission typically takes place when both fighters are on the ground, hence the term ground fighting. Submission techniques primarily stem from Brazilian jiu-jitsu, judo, sambo and catch wrestling. There are many different types of submissions and variants of chokes, arm and leg locks that will force a fighter to verbally or physically submit (tap out), or risk injury. If properly executed, submission techniques are the least dangerous way to finish an opponent in MMA if the subdued fighter is aware of his predicament.

Royce Gracie was the first Brazilian jiu-jitsu stylist in the UFC, and though the style had been around for decades, it was one of the first times fight fans had seen these techniques in action. Gracie's rear naked choke of Ken Shamrock, triangle choke of Dan Severn and simultaneous lapel choke and arm lock of Minoki Ichihara were impressive. Once on the ground, Gracie's opponents appeared defenseless as to what would come next, and soon it was all over. Russian sambo specialist Oleg Taktarov brought leg locks to the UFC early on, and eventually, fighters were doing everything they could to learn how to perform submissions or stay out of them altogether.

The Gracie clan was here to stay, but more Brazilian fighters and teachers came stateside to feed the growing demand of learning submission fighting. Even before there were submission schools in reach, fighter Pat Miletich got his hands on a Renzo Gracie instructional tape, and that served as his first submission foundation. He would literally play the tapes in the gym on a TV and practice with his students.

Brazilian jiu-jitsu students practice in the gi, but after MMA became more popularized with certain rules, "no gi" classes became more prevalent for fighters. The purpose behind the gi was to teach proper positioning first, before the submission attempt; the gi itself can also extend the arm and act as a weapon itself. In Japan, many submission fighters simply bypass positioning and go right for the kill so to speak, which over time, has allowed fighters to experiment as to how they will approach a submission even if they leave themselves open. Japanese fighter Rumina Sato is a good example of this practice, as is Caol Uno and Kazushi Sakuraba.

Like wrestling, many submission practitioners will stick to grappling competitions before making the move into MMA. Travis Lutter is one such example; he won many submission wrestling tournaments and awards before lacing up the gloves. As the money in the sport gets better, more and more BJJ practitioners are making the move, and some still compete in straight grappling to keep their games sharp.

Some of the top submission specialists in MMA include Rodrigo "Minotauro" Nogueira, Frank Mir, Jake Shields, Gilbert Melendez and BJ Penn. Interestingly enough, Eddie Bravo never competed in MMA, earned his BJJ black belt from Jean-Jacques Machado, and created his own move called the Twister. As a brown belt, he defeated Royler Gracie by triangle choke at the 2003 Abu Dhabi Submission Wrestling Championships. Fighters and teachers are still devising new submission techniques which makes this section all that more interesting for fans and students.

In the submission section, TapouT has assembled some of the top submission masters in the world, including: Eddie Bravo, Jean-Jacques Machado, Carlos Machado, Rigan Machado, Nick and Nate Diaz, and a special tribute to the late Jeremy Williams. These techniques cover a wide range of submissions including chokes, arm bars, leg locks and escapes to a submission.

Bobby "Hitman" Pittman is the co-founder of MMA Worldwide. He is a 6 year wrestler with that as his base and a Golden Glove Boxer, 3 Year Blue Belt in Jiu Jitsu under the legend Royce Gracie, a Brown Belt In Kung Fu San Soo under the legend Ron Van Browning. You can contact him at Bobby@MMAWorldwide.com

Bear Hug Escape

Your opponent grabs you from behind.

Grab his right leg with your right hand, to stop him from stepping. With your right leg step behind your opponent.

Pop your hips forward and straighten your upper body. At the same time, throw your right arm into your opponent to force him back. This should be one explosive movement that sweeps your opponent over your right leg.

This is how you should land. Drive your weight into your opponent. Now scissor your legs to go into the sidemount position. From here you can go for a submission, strikes, or just stand up and run, depending on the situation.

Hector Munoz is one of the toughest Brazilian jiu-jitsu fighters in Texas. Earning seven wins in ten fights, Munoz has finished every opponent he has beaten including six submission wins having competed in Ultimate Texas Showdown, Fightfest and Art of War.

Side Mount Arm Bar from Bottom

RJ has Hector in side mount. Hector has his left arm under RJ's neck.

To start creating space Hector shifts his legs to the left.

Here is a look at another angle. Notice Hector's arms are under RJ.

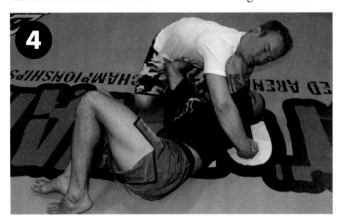

Hector pushes RJ up to create space.

Now Hector elevates his legs . . .

. . . and slides his right knee across RJ's chest and his left leg over his head.

Hector then grips RJ's arm and extends for the finish.

Armbar from Back

1 Hector has RJ's back and has his hands locked under RJ's arms.

2 Releasing his grip, Hector puts his right hand behind RJ's neck.

3 To isolate the arm, Hector brings his left hand to the side of RJ's head.

4 Now Hector begins the armbar. Leaning to his right hip, he pushes RJ's head away with his left arm and controls his arm with his right.

5 With RJ's head pushed to the side, Hector can throw his left leg over his head.

6 Hector then pulls RJ to his back, puts two hands on RJ's right arm . . .

7 . . . and straightens for the armbar finish.

Flying Armbar

RJ and Hector each have a collar tie (hand on their neck) and controlling the other's tricep.

Hector puts his lower shin across the hip of RJ.

Holding RJ's tricep and neck tight, he pulls him to ground.

Once down on the floor, Hector puts his left leg over RJ's head.

To get RJ to the ground Hector pushes with his left leg.

Now RJ is on his side and Hector has his arm controlled.

Hector squeezes his knees together, controls RJ's hand and elevates his hips for the armbar finish.

When Brock Lesnar's camp was looking for a world class BJJ coach they didn't have to go far to find one of the best. Rodrigo Medeiros, or Comprido as he is affectionately called, is considered to be one of the greatest BJJ athletes currently, at the ripe old age of 31. His achievements include being a 7x world champion and one of only four people to ever be crowned world absolute champion twice ('99 and '00). At 16 he began training near his home in Rio de Janeiro and in only five years he was the best in the world. Comprido attributes much of his success to his team, Brasa, whose athletes include Demian Maia and Felipe Costa.

In 2007 Comprido came to Palatine, IL (just outside Chicago) and helped open up Flo MMA. In addition to teaching BJJ at Flo, he performs at seminars around the country, flies to multiple gyms to train UFC fighters, and he also finds time to go to Brazil and teach at a BJJ school for blind children. For more information on Comprido please e-mail info@mataleon.tv.

Rodrigo has his opponent in the butterfly guard and controlling his wrists. His opponent is grabbing his pant legs.

To break the grip, Rodrigo takes his opponent's right sleeve with his right hand and places his left hand under his opponent's hand.

Now all he has to do is pull his opponent's arm across his body.

Rodrigo then grips the back of his opponent's right tricep with both hands and holds it tight to his chest.

Releasing the grip with his left hand, Rodrigo instead grabs the back of his opponent's belt.

With his two holds in place, Rodrigo leans back and begins to elevate his opponent's left leg with his right leg.

Tilting to his side, Rodrigo is able to begin sweeping his opponent to the trapped arm side.

The sweep lands Rodrigo in side mount.

Rodrigo can use the sweep to transition immediately to mount before his opponent has time to settle his position.

Full Guard Sweep to Armbar

Rodrigo has his opponent in full guard.

Using the same grip as technique 2, Rodrigo controls his opponent's right arm . . .

. . . and drags it across his body.

With the right arm secure, Rodrigo reaches over his opponent and grabs his belt.

With the arm and belt secure, Rodrigo begins to lean back.

Rodrigo tilts his weight to his left to open up space.

With that space, Rodrigo scoops up his opponent's left leg with his right arm.

From the opposite angle, Rodrigo kicks his leg over his opponent's body beginning the sweep.

Rodrigo then sweeps his opponent to his back.

Landing in mount, Rodrigo keeps control of his opponent's right arm . . .

. . . to set up the armbar. Rodrigo moves to Z mount with the arm controlled.

He then pulls the arm back for the finish.

Passing the Spider Guard with **Jean Jacques Machado**

by Jean Jacques Machado and Kid Peligro

The spider guard can give fits to even the most experienced jiu-jitsu fighter. Your opponent has control of both sleeves and presses his feet onto your biceps, often changing the angle of his hips and the pressure against your arms to create instability and open various options for sweeps and submission attacks. Circling the hands, as shown in the lesson below, is a quick and effective method to pass. While it is true that the spider guard presents all sorts of difficulties for the attacker, it also has a weakness – both of your opponent's arms and legs are tied up controlling your arms. This weakness can be exploited as shown on page 123. You can also exploit the spider guard when the defender has his legs almost perpendicular to the ground and his feet pointing up – in this case the rollover pass works beautifully. Another good method to pass the spider guard is the leg spin. While some methods of the guard are more difficult to deal with than others, they can all be defeated with proper technique, training, and attention to detail.

The moves in this article were excerpted from "Brazilian Jiu-Jitsu Black Belt Techniques," by Jean Jacques Machado with Kid Peligro, published by Invisible Cities Press. To purchase visit www.BJJmart.com.

Circling the Hands Pass

① Jean Jacques Machado is controlled in the spider guard by his opponent, who controls both sleeves and presses his feet into Jean Jacques' biceps.

② Jean Jacques circles his right hand around his opponent's calf and flicks his elbows up to deflect the left leg. He uses his left hand to grip the pants and push the right leg away.

③ Jean Jacques continues his twisting motion, further moving the opponent's legs away. Notice how Jean Jacques uses his right forearm to drive down the left leg.

④ After clearing all obstacles from his way, Jean Jacques drops down and lands in cross-side control.

⑤ Jean Jacques secures cross-side by passing his right arm around the neck and clamping his chest to his opponent's chest.

Twist Pass

1

Jean Jacques Machado is in the spider guard.

2

Jean Jacques steps back and lifts his opponent's back off the ground.

3

Jean Jacques twists his arms as if he were turning a wheel, breaking the opponent's feet pressure on his biceps.

4

At the end of the spin, the opponent's head is between Jean Jacques' legs and no pressure is on his biceps.

5

Jean Jacques thrusts his hips forward and kneels on his opponent's head. The force of his hips on the arms will force his opponent to release the grip on Jean Jacques' arms.

6

Jean Jacques completes the pass and takes cross-side position.

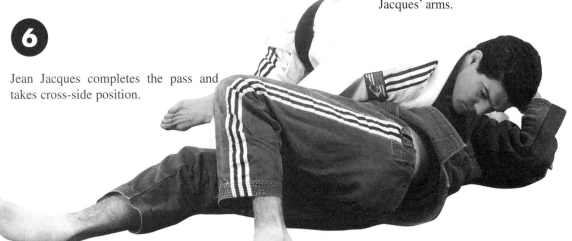

Rousiamr Palhares is currently one of Brazilian Top Team's best fighters. The UFC middleweight is 4-1 in the UFC with three submission finishes. Sporting an 11-2 record, eight of his wins have come by submission with five of them by some type of leg lock proving "Toquiho" is one of the best leg lockers in the game today. A black belt under Brazilian Top Team head Murilo Bustmante, also featured in the techniques, rounds out an impressive submission résumé for the thirty year old fighter.

For more on Palhares, log on to www.braziliantopteam.com.

Heel Hook from Up/Down Position

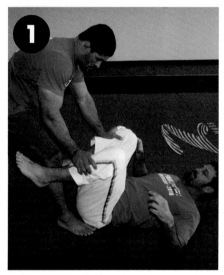

Rousimar is standing above Murilo controlling his legs.

Clinging to Murilo's knee with his right hand, Rousimar closes the gap and stands between Murilo's legs.

Still controlling Murilo's left leg, Rousimar steps his left leg over Murilo to his left side.

Now gripping Murilo's leg with both hands, Rousimar falls back to his right hip.

Now he can attack the heel. Squeezing his knees together for control, Rousimar releases his grip and begins to place his right forearm under Murilo's heel.

Rousimar then grips his hands together tight around Murilo's heel and rotates his body to his left for the finish.

Straight Ankle Lock from Up/Down Position

Rousimar is above Murilo in the up/down position controlling his ankles.

Controling Murilo's left knee with his right hand, Rousimar steps in between Murilo's legs.

Rousimar pushes Murilo's right foot away using his left, free hand so Murilo can not use it to defend.

Now Rousimar is free to fall back on his hip while sliding his grip down around the shin of Murilo.

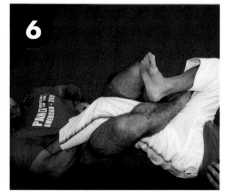

Rousimar then plants his right foot on the mat between Murilo's legs and arches back.

Here is a closer look. Rousimar uses his right foot to elevate Murilo's right leg.

Now he can cross his legs with his right foot under his left.

With the position secure, Rousimar can grip his hands together, arch back and finish the straight ankle lock.

Manny Tapia is the current King of the Cage World Champion at 135 lbs. Manny fights out of Millennia Jiu-Jitsu. For more info on training with Manny and his teammates visit www.millenniajiujitsu.com.

Inverted Heel Hook from Side Mount

Manny Tapia has the side mount on Romie Aram.

Romie brings his right arm inside and pushes against Manny's hips. This helps Romie scoot his hips away and create the space needed to escape.

Manny brings his right leg up to give Romie some space. This tricks Romie into thinking he should try to put Manny into his guard, so Romie brings his right leg across.

As soon as Romie's leg comes up Manny traps it with his right leg as shown here. Manny also uses his right arm to trap Romie's foot against his hip.

Now, Manny sits back for the heel hook, wrapping his right arm around Romie's foot.

Manny locks his hands and forces his right arm across his chest to twist Romie's ankle for the inverted heel hook. Notice how Manny squeezes his knees together to help control Romie's leg.

Arm Bar from Side Mount

Manny has Mac Danzig in the side mount.

Manny scissors his hips, putting his right hip to the mat, to create space.

Now, Manny reaches under Mac's right arm.

Manny brings his right leg up to the knee-on-stomach position. Notice how Manny has both hands out for base.

Manny brings his left arm over Mac's head and uses his chest / weight to force Mac's right arm down.

Manny swings his left leg around Mac's head to go for the arm bar. Manny uses his right arm to keep Mac's right arm trapped against his chest.

Manny brings his left leg around until it is right next to Mac's head.

Now, Manny sits back for the arm bar.

Manny traps Mac's arm against his chest with both arms and pushes his hips straight up to finish the arm bar. Manny also squeezes his knees together to help control Mac's arm.

Like many, Javier Vazquez began his training in high school, where he started wrestling at age 15. Unlike many, Javier went on to become one of the most talented fighters and trainers in the world. Since he started training BJJ with Rodrigo Medeiros, Javier has earned the rank of black belt and won numerous tournaments across the globe. Javier was also one of the founding members of Millennia Jiu-Jitsu alongside Romie Aram and John Jensen. Now, Javier is teaching at the Javier Jiu-Jitsu Academy in La Habra, CA and if you ever get the chance you should check it out. For more info on Javier and how to train with him, go to www.showtimejiujitsu.com and be sure to check out Javier's DVDs on Mastering Grappling.

Getting the Hooks In from Rear Mount

Javier has the rear mount on Charles. Javier's left knee is on the ground next to Charles' right knee and Javier's right foot is up. Javier locks his arms around Charles' head and left arm.

Keeping his arms locked, Javier rolls onto his left shoulder and pulls Charles over.

Javier continues to roll until he ends up on his back. Notice how Javier kept Charles' body tight against his chest throughout the entire roll.

Once they finish the roll, Javier throws his right leg inside Charles' right leg (right hook in).

Here is another angle of position 4. Notice that Javier has his right hook in and still has his arms locked around Charles' head and arm.

Now, Javier posts his head on the ground and comes up onto his left knee.

Here you can see how Javier is now on his left knee.

Javier rolls to his right side, pulling Charles with him.

Here you can see how Javier rolls to the right.

Javier continues to roll until he can bring his left leg through.

Now, Javier throws his left hook in. Both hooks are now in and Javier can go for the choke with his arms while still controlling Charles with his legs.

Counter to your Opponent's Choke Defenses - Rear Naked Choke

Javier has Charles' back with both hooks in. Javier wants to go for the choke with his right arm, but he doesn't want Charles to trap it.

Instead of going straight for the choke, Javier grabs Charles' right arm.

Javier passes Charles' right arm to his left hand. Javier also traps Charles' left arm.

Javier brings his right foot over Charles' right arm to trap it.

Javier grabs his right foot with his left hand and pulls it in tight.

Now, Javier brings his left leg up and locks his legs, securing Charles' right arm.

Javier reaches inside and grabs Charles' left arm with his left hand.

Now that Javier has both arms trapped he can go for the choke with his right arm. He wraps it around Charles' neck...

...then quickly brings his left arm up and locks the rear naked choke, squeezing for the submission.

The 2nd oldest son of Helio Gracie, Relson Gracie moved to Hawaii in 1988. He began learning jiu-jitsu at age 2 and entered his first competition at the tender age of 10! He was the Brazilian National Champion for 22 years straight, and during this period went undefeated. He became so popular that he attained the nickname "Campeao" or "Champion" among his friends and fans. Upon his arrival to Honolulu, it was with great pleasure that Relson introduced the art of Gracie Jiu-jitsu to the Aloha State. Now retired from competition, Relson continues to enjoy teaching classes in Hawaii and has become quite fond of the island life. For more info on Relson and how you can train with him, visit www.relsongracie.com.

Arm Bar from the Guard

Relson Gracie has Imiola Lindsey in his open guard. Relson has his right hand inside the collar and his left hand grabs the back of Imiola's right arm. Relson keeps his left foot on Imiola's hip and he uses his right foot to block Imiola from striking with his left hand.

Imiola stands up to try and pass the guard.

Notice how Relson keeps his right foot against Imiola's left arm in case he tries to punch.

Now, Relson puts both feet on Imiola's hips.

Relson pulls Imiola's torso down with his arms and pushes Imiola's hips up with his legs.

Here you can see how Relson elevates Imiola.

Once Imiola is elevated, Relson brings his left leg out and swings it around Imiola's head, letting him fall into an arm bar. Notice how Relson keeps his right foot on Imiola's hip. This is crucial to making Imiola fall into the arm bar.

Imiola lands flat on his back in an arm bar.

Relson squeezes his legs together and raises his hip to finish the arm bar. Relson also makes sure that Imiola's thumb is pointing up to make the arm bar more effective.

Taking Your Opponent's Back for the Choke

Relson has Imiola in his guard. With his left hand, Relson grabs the gi behind Imiola's right arm. With his right hand, Relson grabs the gi by Imiola's right wrist.

Relson uses both hands to drag Imiola's arm across his body.

Now, Relson sits up and bases himself on his right elbow. With his left hand, he reaches around Imiola's body and grabs his right wrist.

Relson pulls himself onto Imiola's back and puts both hooks inside Imiola's legs. Notice how Relson posts his right hand on the mat to help push himself up.

Now that he has his hooks in, Relson rolls to his right side and pulls Imiola with him. Notice that he doesn't let go of Imiola's wrist.

Relson continues to roll, pulling Imiola on top of him.

As soon as they roll over, Relson wraps his right arm around Imiola's neck.

With his left hand, Relson reaches underneath Imiola's left arm and feeds the collar to his right hand.

With his left arm still under Imiola's left arm, Relson reaches behind Imiola's head. Relson pushes forward with his left hand and pulls the collar across Imiola's neck with his right hand to finish the choke.

The Jean Jacques Machado black belt started training BJJ in May 1994, and now instructs at his 10th Planet Jiu-Jitsu Academy in Hollywood, California. Bravo won the Abu Dhabi North American Trials lightweight division on October 5, 2002, in San Diego, California, earning the Most Technical Fighter Of The Night award and went onto the 2003 Abu Dhabi Championships in San Paulo, Brazil, where he secured a submission win over legendary Royler Gracie. By the time you read this Eddie should be moved into the Legends MMA Training Center along with Randy Couture, Bas Rutten and many others. Be sure to check the website, www.legendsmma.com, for the grand opening and Eddie's class schedule. For more info you can also go to Eddie's website at www.thetwister.tv or contact him on MySpace at www.myspace.com/thetwister.

Loco Plata from the Mount

1 Eddie has the mount on Peter. Peter wraps his arms around Eddie's waist and pulls himself tight against Eddie's body so there is no room for Eddie to strike.

2 Eddie swings his left leg around towards Peter's head. Notice how Eddie has Peter's right arm trapped.

3 Eddie continues to bring his left leg around until he ends up here.

4 Now, Eddie brings his right arm across, pushing Peter's head away with his forearm.

5 Eddie uses his right arm to help lift his foot over Peter's head.

6 Eddie turns his body and drops his left hip to the mat to bring his left leg across Peter's neck.

7 With his left arm, Eddie reaches around Peter's neck.

8 Eddie grabs his foot with his left hand, pulling it into Peter's neck. He also uses his right hand to help push his foot down, making sure that it is under Peter's chin.

9 Once Eddie has the lock in place he uses his right hand to control Peter's left arm with wrist control.

10 Eddie brings his right leg up and places his right foot on top of his left. Eddie pulls with his left arm and pushes both feet into Peter's neck to finish the choke.

SEE PAGE 176 FOR AN EXCLUSIVE MMA WORLDWIDE PACKAGE DEAL!

Loco Plata - Counter to the Counter

Eddie has the mount on Peter. Peter wraps his arms around Eddie's waist and pulls himself tight against Eddie's body so there is no room for Eddie to strike.

Eddie swings his left leg around towards Peter's head. Notice how Eddie has Peter's right arm trapped.

Now, Eddie brings his right arm across, pushing Peter's head away with his forearm.

Eddie uses his right arm to help lift his foot over Peter's head.

Eddie turns his body and drops his left hip to the mat to bring his left leg across Peter's neck. Peter will counter the move by rolling to his right.

Here you can see how Peter counters the move by rolling. Notice how Eddie keeps his left arm against his left leg, so Peter can't pull his arm out.

Peter continues to roll until he is on both knees. Eddie immediately pulls his foot in front of Peter's face, going for the same move, just from the bottom.

Eddie gets his shin / foot across Peter's neck. He reaches around Peter's neck with his left arm and grabs his foot to lock up the choke. Notice how Eddie also uses his right hand to push his foot into Peter's neck.

Now, that he has the choke locked in, Eddie uses his right hand to control Peter's left arm with wrist control so he can't strike.

Eddie brings his right leg in, pushing his right foot into his left heel. He also pulls down with his left arm to help finish the choke.

Loco Plata Attempt to Oma Plata

From this position Eddie also has the option of going for the Oma Plata. Notice again how Eddie keeps his left arm wrapped around his left knee so Peter can't pull his arm out. This is crucial to the success of the move.

Eddie uses his right hand to help push his left leg across Peter's face. Eddie wants to spin his body to the left and bring his left foot to the mat.

Here you can see how Eddie spins his body to the left and brings his left foot down to the mat. Notice how Eddie uses his right hand to keep Peter's arm trapped.

Eddie keeps spinning until he can cross his left leg under his right leg. He also continues to hold Peter's arm with his right hand.

Now, Eddie starts to sit up.

Here you can see how Eddie has Peter's arm trapped. Notice how Eddie also wraps his left arm around Peter's waist to keep him from doing a forward roll for the escape.

Eddie brings his right leg out to the side so he can sit up farther.

Eddie reaches under Peter's chest with his right arm and pulls himself forward which raises Peter's arm even more for the submission.

Ground and Pound Defense with **Paulo "Junior" Gazze**

Paulo "Junior" Gazze is a Brazilian jiu-jitsu black belt from Sao Paulo, Brazil. He has won several tournaments in jiu-jitsu including a Pan American Championship. A regular in the Huntington Beach, California training circuit, Junior has trained with the likes of Tito Ortiz, Ricco Rodriguez, Jason Miller, "Razor" Rob McCullough, Quinton Jackson and Michael Bisping. As owner and head coach of the Gazze Academy in Huntington Beach, Junior is teaching his own team and sharing his vast knowledge of MMA and jiu-jitsu.

For more on Junior and the Gazze Academy, log on to www.hbbjj.com.

Triangle Choke

Junior is on his back with Jason in his guard punching. Junior is protecting his head.

To keep from getting punched, Junior controls Jason's biceps . . .

. . . and pulls him in close so Jason can no longer punch from a postured position.

Junior posts his left leg on the mat and shifts his hips out to his left while still controlling Jason's arm.

Junior takes Jason's left arm and drives it behind his back, switching to his left hand . . .

. . . and hooking his left foot under Jason's left arm.

With Jason's arm secure, Junior releases his grip so he can switch hands.

Jason now is completely immobile and trapped.

Junior can either strike with his right hand or apply a triangle choke.

Carlos Machado is a 7th Degree Black Belt in Brazilian Jiu-Jitsu. He is the eldest of the Machado Brothers, and operates his academy (Machado Jiu-Jitsu Dallas) at 13881 Midway Rd. Suite #104, Farmers Branch, Texas. He also runs a fast growing BJJ Association and offers seminar and instructional DVDs. For more information, please call 972-934-1316, or send email to jiu-jitsu@sbcglobal.net. His website address is www.carlosmachado.net.

Crossmount Armbar Set Up

Carlos starts with cross face and far elbow control from the right side.

Carlos sets up his right knee on the stomach of his opponent with his left leg posted. His opponent tries to push the knee off his stomach with his left hand.

Carlos grabs with his right arm inside his opponent's left elbow.

Carlos then steps his left leg over his partner's head and maintains tight arm control.

Carlos spins his hip towards the left side and sits on the mat. With his left hand Carlos grabs his opponent's left leg to keep him from rolling. Carlos pulls down with his right hand and raises his hips to finish the armbar.

Armbar Counter Against Standing Front Choke

Carlos' opponent attacks his neck while Carlos grabs both of his opponent's elbows.

Carlos side steps with his left leg and posts his right foot above his opponent's left knee.

Carlos sits back with his left foot on the floor, and stretches out his right leg, pushing his opponents' leg back.

Carlos lets go of his opponent's left arm and turns his body facing the mat. Notice how Carlos traps his opponent's arm with his left hand.

Carlos steps his left leg over his opponent's head and locks in the armbar. Now, Carlos pushes his hips forward and pulls back with his arms for the submission.

SEE PAGE 176 FOR AN EXCLUSIVE MMA WORLDWIDE PACKAGE DEAL!

John is the youngest of five brothers of the world-renowned Machado Brazilian Jiu-Jitsu martial arts family. Born in Rio De Janeiro, Brazil, John began his jiu-jitsu training over twenty years ago. Dominating the competitive arena of Brazilian Jiu-Jitsu in his native country, seizing every major title and competitive award from 1982-1990, John holds the prestigious rank of 4th degree black belt in BJJ.

As one of the most admired and respected BJJ practitioners in the world today, John is recognized not only for his outstanding competitive accomplishments, but also for his teaching expertise. He is in demand throughout the world as one of the foremost authorities on martial arts. John's talent has also been showcased in a variety of television shows and major motion pictures.

For more info on John and training with him visit his website at www.johnmachado.net.

Option 1 - Choke from Front Headlock

John has a front headlock on Peter. His left arm is around Peter's neck and his hands are locked behind Peter's left arm.

John sits onto his butt, bringing his right leg straight out.

John hooks his right leg over Peter's left leg to help maintain control.

Now, John rocks back and to the left and pulls into Peter's throat for the choke.

Notice how John dips his left shoulder down to get a tighter wrap around Peter's neck.

Option 2 - Anaconda Choke with Leg Hooked

Once John gets to this position, he has a few more options. He has his right leg hooked over Peter's left leg to help control him.

Just as the last move, John rolls to his left for the choke.

If Peter tries to escape, John can use his right leg to control Peter's left leg, not allowing him to base up.

Sometimes in this position your choke may not be tight enough to submit some opponents.

John will lock his left hand on his right bicep, then reach across Peter's back with his right hand and squeeze for the Anaconda choke.

Option 3 - Anaconda Choke - Elevating the Leg

Now, we go to the third variation from this position. Peter does his best to maintain a solid base, not allowing John to roll to his side for the finish.

Instead of hooking with his right leg, John puts it inside Peter's left leg and uses it to elevate Peter and roll him to his side.

Here you can see how John elevates the leg and rolls Peter over.

Same as before, John locks up the Anaconda and squeezes for the submission.

Option 4 - Crucifix

Here we are again in the same position. This time Peter tries to push into John and fight his way out of the hold.

Here you can see how Peter starts to push forward. John immediately hooks Peter's left leg with his right leg and starts rolling to his right side.

Here you can see how John rolls Peter over. He used an under hook with his left arm and an over hook with his right arm.

John continues to roll until he comes up onto his knees. Notice how John's left leg went over Peter's left arm. Also notice that John kept the under hook with his left arm.

John locks his hands together to maintain control of Peter's right arm. Now, John leans his body into Peter for the neck crank.

Antonio Rodrigo Nogueira is one of the best Brazilian Jiu Jitsu artists in MMA. A successful career in PrideFC saw the heavyweight submit the likes of Mark Coleman, Dan Henderson and Mirko "Cro Cop" Filipovic as well as earn a heavyweight belt. His accomplishments in Japan grabbed the attention of the UFC where he made a successful debut with a win over Heath Herring at UFC 73. For more on Nogueira look for him in issue four of *MMA Worldwide Magazine*.

Log on to www.minotauro.net for more on Antonio.

Oma Plata to Arm Bar

Nogueira has Freddy in his full guard.

Nogueira goes for a kimura on Freddy's left arm.

The kimura is used as a set up. Nogueira maintains control of Freddy's left wrist and pushes Freddy's head away with his left hand.

Nogueira then brings his right leg over Freddy's shoulder and bends Freddy's left arm.

Nogueira brings his left leg up to figure 4 Freddy's shoulder.

Nogueira adjusts his grip to...

...straighten Freddy's arm out for an arm bar.

Nogueira posts his right hand on Freddy's leg.

He then rotates his hips across Freddy's elbow and extends his hips finishing the hold.

SEE PAGE 176 FOR AN EXCLUSIVE MMA WORLDWIDE PACKAGE DEAL!

Cross Arm Arm-Bar

Nogueira has Freddy in his full guard.

Nogueira pulls Freddy into him with his hips and goes for an under hook with his left arm.

He then locks his hands.

Nogueira rotates his hips outward.

Nogueira tries to bring his head outside of Freddy's arm.

Freddy brings his elbow up to defend so Nogueira goes for Freddy's far arm while still maintaining a grip on his near arm.

Nogueira brings Freddy's arm across his body tightening the pressure.

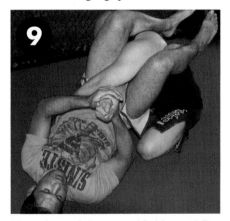

He rotates his hips to the side and brings his left leg over the head of Freddy.

He straightens out his hips and finishes the arm bar.

Undefeated Caesar Gracie Jiu Jitsu fighter, Gilbert Melendez has made a huge splash in the lightweight division. Ranked 3rd in the MMA Worldwide Rankings, Melendez's aggressive kickboxing style mixed with relentless ground work have given Gilbert twelve consecutive wins with only four going the distance. The Strikeforce lightweight champion had his biggest win ever against highly touted Tatsuya Kawajiri in Pride's New Year's Eve show in 2006. Look for Melendez to continue his dominance over Strikeforce's lightweight division.

Turtle Attack to Side Choke

Gilbert is on top of Alex Serdyukov who is in the turtle position.

Gilbert locks up Alex's far head and arm and starts to sag his hips to his right side.

Gilbert roles Alex to his back while maintaining the hold.

Using his right foot as leverage, Gilbert slides Alex's weight off of him.

Gilbert slides his right foot in between Alex's legs for leverage to...

...turn to his stomach trapping Alex's right arm and head.

Here is a closer look on the hold.

Gilbert slides his right leg out, figure fours his arms and finishes the choke.

Side Choke to Triangle Choke

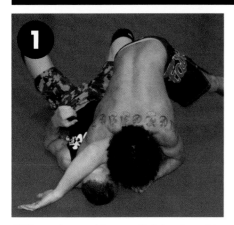

Gilbert is unable to finish the side choke.

He releases the hold, brings his left knee to Alex's right shoulder and posts his left hand.

Using his right hand Gilbert lifts up Alex's head to...

...bring his right leg over Alex's left shoulder and under his head.

Gilbert grabs his own right ankle.

Then posts his right hand for support.

Now Gilbert can bring his right ankle under his left leg for the triangle.

Gilbert sits back into position...

and lifts up Alex's head for the finish.

Knee on Stomach to Kimura

Gilbert is on top of Alex with his knee on his stomach and Alex's left arm under hooked.

Gilbert posts his left hand on Alex's head.

Gilbert steps over Alex's head with his left foot.

Gilbert sits his weight on Alex's head.

He then kneels down trapping Alex's right arm with his right shin.

Now Gilbert can turn his attention to Alex's left arm.

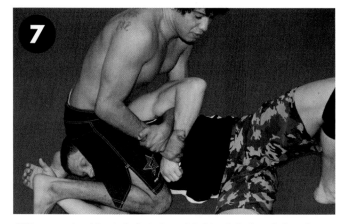

Gilbert grabs Alex's left wrist with his right hand then loops his left arm under Alex's arm and grabs his own wrist for the Kimura.

Gilbert then brings Alex's arm to his back, driving Alex's wrist to the back of his neck finishing the submission.

Guard Pass to Sidemount

Here is a simple but effective guard pass.

Gilbert pushes on Alex's ribs and slides his hips back creating space.

Gilbert then brings both his arms under Alex's thighs. Be careful to avoid getting put in a triangle.

Gilbert locks his hands around both of Alex's legs.

Gilbert lifts his head up elevating Alex's hips.

Gilbert brings his left arm across Alex's body, drives his left knee over Alex and rotates his hips inward.

Now Gilbert can clear Alex's legs off his body.

Sagging his hips, Gilbert can now settle on Alex's side.

Gilbert then turns into Alex into a side mount.

Renato "Babalu" Sobral is one of Gracie Barra Combat Team's most elite fighters, training with the likes of Marcio Feitosa, Ebenezer Fontes Braga, and Marcio Cruz. The Rio De Janeiro native has amassed huge wins over quality opponents including Mauricio "Shogun" Rua and Jeremy Horn. His aggressive style, along with slick submissions, has pushed Babaula into the upper echelon of fighters. Here are some of the techniques that put Babalu up with the elite.

Half Guard to Back

Babalu has his opponent in his half guard. Notice his left hand on his opponent's right tricep.

Babalu clears his opponent's right arm, slides his hips out to the right and brings his head and shoulders out from under his opponent.

He then posts his left hand and grabs his opponent's thigh as leverage to bring his hips out front more.

Babalu then brings his left knee out and moves his right arm over the back of his opponent.

He then brings his right foot through his opponent's legs and starts to bring his left leg around.

Babalu then rotates around his opponent preparing to take his back.

He then puts both hooks in...

...and finishes with the choke.

BJ Penn is one of the most successful Brazilian Jiu Jitsu practitioners in MMA today. As the first non-Brazilian to win the Jiu Jitsu World Championships, Penn has combined slick submissions, heavy hands and a tough wrestling game into a stellar MMA career. With wins over Matt Hughes, Takanori Gomi and Renzo Gracie just to name a few, BJ's skills are unquestionable.

From BJ Penn's Victory Belt Book, Mixed Martial Arts: The Book of Knowledge, available at www.victorybelt.com and bookstores everywhere.

Triangle Arm Bar from the Back

BJ has Beach's back sitting up right with wrist control.

As BJ falls to his right he begins forcing Beach's left arm to his hips with his left hand.

With Beach's left arm down towards BJ's waist he can now begin to maneuver his left leg over Beach's left arm.

BJ can now bring his left leg over Beach's left arm, trapping it to his waist.

Beach now turns to avoid trouble so BJ brings his left leg over Beach's left shoulder. Notice BJ is constantly squeezing his legs to keep from getting swept.

BJ then puts a figure four around Beach's head and arm securing the reverse triangle. He also hooks Beach's right arm.

BJ then extends Beach's right arm by latching onto it and extending to his back.

With Beach flat on his back, BJ can release his left leg and bring it over Beach's head.

To finish BJ pulls Beach's arm to his chest, squeezes his legs tight and elevates his hips.

The 22 year old Nam Phan is a Jiu Jitsu specialist and one of MMA Worldwide's Top 50 Most Exciting Fighters of All Time. Riding a seven fight win streak, the California native ran into back to back losses against tough lightweights Josh Thomson and Gesias "JZ" Calvancante. Back on the winning track, the lightweight notched a win over Shad Smith.

Nam demonstrates his moves with his past coach, the late Jeremy Williams of Apex Jiu Jitsu.

Front Head Lock Escape to Sweep

Jeremy has Nam in a front headlock.

Nam reaches up with his right arm around Jeremy's waist.

Posting on his left hand, Nam scoots his hips in close to Jeremy looking for a butterfly hook.

With his right butterfly hook, Nam elevates Jeremy's left leg and reaches for Jeremy's other leg with his left hand.

Here is a look at another angle. Notice Nam has both legs wrapped up with his arms.

Nam pinches Jeremy's legs together so...

...he can get his hips over Jeremy's legs.

By trapping Jeremy's legs he keeps Jeremy from pulling guard. With his left knee tight against the opposite side of Jeremy...

...Nam can move to side mount.

Butterfly Sweep to Side Mount

Jeremy is in Nam's butterfly guard.

Pushing on Jeremy's neck, Nam creates space with his arms.

Continuing to push with his right hand, Nam posts with his left hand and scoots his hips to his right.

Nam moves his hand from Jeremy's neck to an under hook.

Nam traps Jeremy's right arm in an over hook.

Leaning his weight to his left, Nam elevates Jeremy's left leg with his butterfly hook.

This brings Jeremy to his back.

Nam quickly establishes his base by posting with his feet.

Nam slides his right leg under his body keeping Jeremy from pulling guard. He ends up in a side mount.

World Extreme Cagefighting regular Cub Swanson is no stranger to submissions. Training under the legendary Erik Paulson, Cub is dangerous on the ground and on his feet. His flexibility and long limbs provide excellent tools for his crafty tricks on the ground. For more on Cub log on to www.cubswanson.com.

Triangle from Back

Cub has Cory's back with his hooks in.

Cub releases his left hook, starts to slide off to the right and grips Cory's left wrist.

Here is another angle. Notice he has his free foot and hand based out.

Now Cub begins to slide his right leg far under Cory's armpit.

With his hip on the mat now, Cub brings his right leg around Cory's neck.

Cub slides to his back now while maintaining his hold on Cory.

Now Cub can bring his left leg over his right foot to lock in the triangle choke.

To tighten the hold, Cub uses both hands to pull Cory's left arm towards him.

Cub pulls with his arms and elevates his hips to finish the choke.

Kimura Lock Variation

Cub is on top ready to execute a kimura but Cory is defending.

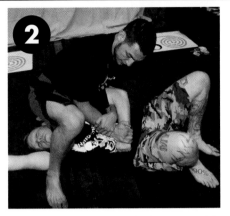

So Cub steps over Cory's right arm with his right foot.

Cub releases his right hand and brings his leg behind Cory's head using his right hand to push his head up.

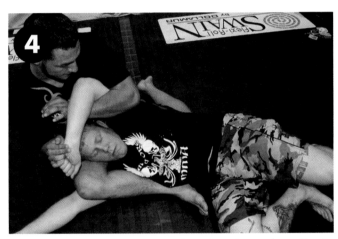

Leaning back, Cub drives his right leg deeper into Cory's neck.

Now Cub can lock in a reverse triangle.

With his new hold Cub can now go back to attacking the arm.

He can either attack the shoulder by pulling back on Cory's elbow.

Or he can lock up the kimura hold again, rotate Cory's arm outward and finish.

Jeremy Williams was a product of both Marco Ruas and Chris Brennan. While his Muay Thai was top notch, Jeremy preferred to submit his opponents with six of seven of his wins coming by way of submission. After a five year lay off, Jeremy returned to fighting making his IFL debut for Marco Ruas' Condors in January of 2007. In his gym, Apex Jiu Jitsu, Jeremy showed us some of the moves that made him a top instructor.

Even after his passing, Jeremy's talents continue to inspire and contribute to the sport.

D'Arce Choke in Half Guard

Jeremy is in Nam's half guard. Nam has an under hook and is looking to escape.

Posting his left foot out, Jeremy slides his right arm under Nam's neck.

Jeremy grips his left hand with his right.

With his grip secure Jeremy pulls Nam's head up.

Now Jeremy pinches his elbows together bringing his left forearm down pushing Nam's head.

Jeremy then slides his left arm down across Nam's back then grabs his left bicep with his right hand.

To finish, Jeremy pinches his elbows together and drops his hips.

Guillotine Choke in Half Guard

Jeremy is in Nam's half guard. Nam has an under hook and is looking to escape.

Posting his left foot out, Jeremy slides his right arm under Nam's neck.

Jeremy grips his left hand with his right.

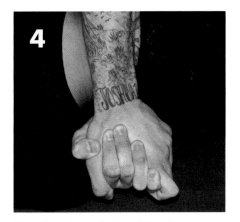

Here is a closer look at his grip.

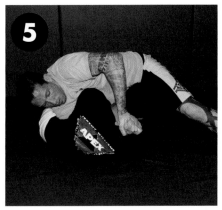

With his grip secure Jeremy pulls Nam's head up.

Now Jeremy pinches his elbows together bringing his right forearm across Nam's neck.

Jeremy then traps Nam's right leg by figure fouring his own legs.

This prevents Nam from escaping and tightens the hold.

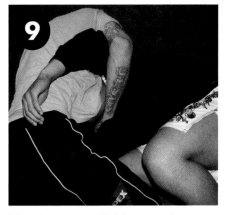

Now Jeremy can finish the choke.

Arm in Guillotine Choke Variation

Jeremy has Nam in a front head and arm lock.

Jeremy circles to his right, maintains his grip and slides his left forearm to the back of Nam's neck.

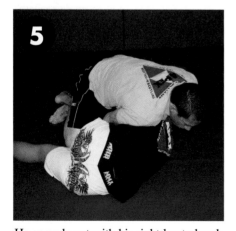

Now Jeremy comes in tight to Nam's left side.

Jeremy steps over Nam's left leg with his right.

He sprawls out with his right leg to break Nam down to his hips.

Jeremy then figure four's his legs to keep Nam from escaping.

Now Jeremy can finish the same choke from Technique 2.

Anaconda Choke Variation

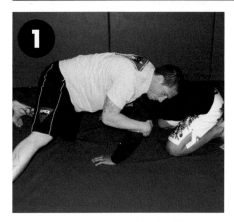

1

Jeremy has a front head lock. Chin control with his left hand and tricep control with his right hand.

2

Pushing Nam's left arm across his neck, Jeremy starts to bring his left hand under Nam's left arm pit.

3

Jeremy then grabs his right bicep with his left hand.

4

Now Jeremy grabs his left elbow with his right hand.

5

Here is a closer look of the hold.

6

With his grip secure, Jeremy posts up on his feet.

7

Jeremy brings his hips in tight to Nam with his left shin across Nam's hips.

8

Now Jeremy brings his right leg over the back of Nam and arches his back finishing the choke.

9

Here is a final look of the choke.

SEE PAGE 176 FOR AN EXCLUSIVE MMA WORLDWIDE PACKAGE DEAL!

Dean "The Boogie Man" Lister is one of the most respected submission artists in the UFC today. An absolute champion in the world renowned Abu Dhabi Championships and a US National Sambo Champion, Lister is on the short list of prestigious American grapplers. Currently fighting in the UFC middleweight division, Lister has won four out of five in the UFC and is in the hunt for the title. Currently living and teaching in San Diego, you can train with Dean at Xtreme Couture San Diego. Log on to www.xtremecouture.tv or www.deanlister.com.

Counter to Straight Ankle Lock – Heel Hook

Dean's opponent is going for a straight ankle lock with his right foot hooking Dean's left leg.

With his palms facing his opponent, Dean brings his left hand under and his right hand over his opponent's right leg.

Dean locks his hands in a tight Gable grip.

Pressuring hard with his right elbow, Dean drives his opponent's right knee to the ground.

Now Dean can pull his opponent's foot out from under his leg . . .

. . . and slide his grip to the heel for the heel hook.

Leg Lock Defense

Heel Hook Counters (1)

Dean's opponent is attempting a heel hook on Dean's right leg. Notice his right heel is under Dean and exposed.

Countering, Dean grips his opponent's heel with both hands.

Keeping the foot tight beneath him, Dean pulls up hard on his opponent's heel. His opponent will either let go and scramble out of the hold or risk ligament damage.

Heel Hook Counters (2)

Dean's opponent is attempting a heel hook on Dean's right leg. Notice his opponent has his left foot crossed underneath his right leg.

Dean yanks his opponent's left foot out from under his right leg . . .

. . . and gets a reverse heel hook on his opponent. (While both fighters have heel hooks, Dean's is a superior position.)

Caesar Gracie is one of the most sought after and successful Jiu Jitsu coaches in the United States. He has coached some of California's most successful fighters including Nick Diaz, Nathan Diaz and Jake Shields. As of September 16th, these three fighters have a combined 48 – 13 record with 20 submissions. These three, along with several other Bay Area fighters, make up team Eternal Unlimited based out of San Francisco, CA.

Heel Hook from Half Guard with Jake Shields

Jake starts off in Dan's half guard.

To start, Jake places a firm grip, not a squeeze, on Dan's throat to push him to the mat and to use for leverage.

With his one hand on Dan's throat and the other on his leg, Jake starts to fall back and swing his right leg around Dan's left leg.

Jake now has his leg hooked around Dan's and his side to the mat.

Jake is pinching his legs tightly around Dan's leg to keep the pressure tight on his knee.

Now Jake posts his left hand and scoots himself back and begins to swing his right around to secure the heel hook.

Jake now has the blade of his right forearm under Dan's heel with Dan's foot tucked under his armpit.

Here Jake is showing us the correct angle to crank the heel hook.

Jake finishes the heel hook here by applying pressure in an upward direction and forces Dan to tap.

Armbar from Closed Guard

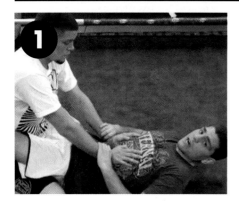

Nick is starting off with Nathan in his closed guard, and gripping both of Nathan's wrists.

Nick slides his right hand under Nathan's left arm and secures his grip behind Nathan's right elbow.

Nick breaks Nathan's posture down by pulling Nate's right arm across Nick's body and pulling him down with his legs.

Nick now has Nathan's posture broken with his guard high up on Nathan's back and his right arm secured.

Nick now reaches around Nathan's back and grips his left armpit with his right hand, while still securing his right elbow.

Nick now slides his left elbow around Nathan's head to cross face him.

Nick now has Nathan cross faced. From here he will hit the armbar in one move so as not to further telegraph it.

Nick pushes Nathan further off posture with his right leg and swings his left leg around Nathan's head.

Nick now lifts his hips and straightens Nathan's arm to finish the armbar.

Simple Sweep with Nathan Diaz

Nathan starts off with Jason posturing up in his closed guard.

Nathan then grabs behind Jason's elbow with his left hand and grabs behind Jason's neck with his right hand.

Nathan then breaks his open guard and plants his right foot on the mat while still holding Jason securely.

Nathan then swivels his hips out to get his right knee across Jason's hips and his left leg to the mat.

It is very important to make sure your left leg is on the mat like Nathan's here, so that he can chop Jason's leg out.

Nathan then pulls Jason on top of him to start the sweep.

Nathan then "chops" out Jason's right leg and turns his body toward the mat, while pulling Jason's right elbow in.

Nathan makes sure his right leg is clear when performing the sweep so that he can end in the mount position.

Nathan finishes the Simple Sweep in the mount position.

SEE PAGE 176 FOR AN EXCLUSIVE MMA WORLDWIDE PACKAGE DEAL!

Gogoplata from Double Leg Takedown with Nick Diaz

1 Nathan just took Nick down with a double leg and is holding him tight so he cannot escape.

2 As soon as Nick hits the mat he is working to push Nathan's head to his left side and swing his right leg over Nate's left shoulder.

3 Once Nick has his leg over Nathan's shoulder he grabs his ankle with his left hand and pulls his leg downwards so he can slip his shin under Nathan's chin for the choke.

4 Nick let's go of Nathan's head with his right hand and slips the very bottom of his shin under Nathan's chin and flexes his foot upwards hooking Nathan's neck.

5 If Nathan were to turn his head away from the choke, Nick would counter with the Omoplata.

6 Nick then grabs Nathan's head with his right hand and grabs his wrist with his left hand so he can slip his left leg out to secure the figure four and finish the choke.

7 While holding Nathan's wrist with his left hand, Nick slips his left leg out.

8 Nick locks the figure four with his legs and grabs his left leg with his right hand and pulls down to finish the choke. This is one way to finish the Gogoplata.

9 The other way to finish the Gogoplata is to grab the head with both hands and pull down like Nick is doing here.

Triangle from Closed Guard

Gilbert is blocking a strike from his opponent who is in his closed guard.

Gilbert blocks the next strike his opponent throws and starts to over hook his arm.

Gilbert secures the over hook and begins to bring his opponent close to his chest.

Now Gilbert grabs the back of his opponent's head and pulls him down to his chest, while still securing his right arm. Everything is tight.

From this position, Gilbert's opponent starts to throw strikes. Gilbert blocks the strike with his forearm.

Gilbert now pushes his opponents left arm towards his shin, opens his guard and brings his knees up.

Gilbert now secures his opponents left arm against his shin by holding his tricep tight to his shin.

This whole time Gilbert has secured his opponent's right arm. He now slides his hand down to his opponent's wrist to start the triangle.

Gilbert brings his right leg around to secure the triangle and from here he can rain down elbows or lock his figure four and finish the triangle.

Heel Hook Variation

Jake starts off with his feet hooked behind Ryan's knees, with Ryan standing above him.

Jake now grabs Ryan's left heel and shoots his right leg through as far as he can.

When Jake shoots his leg through, he grabs the mat with his heel and pulls his body as deep as he can under Ryan's legs.

He now swings his right leg around Ryan's hip and places his foot on Ryan's chest securing Ryan's fight leg.

Jake kicks out Ryan's left leg with his free leg and pushes him back with his right foot. Jake is also securing Ryan's left leg under his arm pit.

When Ryan falls to the mat Jake feeds his right foot under his left heel. He does this so Ryan cannot grab his heel for a heel hook or spin out.

Jake is bending Ryan's knee and arching back to create the most tension possible for the heel hook as he slides his hand under Ryan's heel.

Jake now grips his right hand with his left and lifts up towards his own head to finish the heel hook.

Here Jake shows us if Ryan tucks his heel to prevent the heel hook, Jake can also push his toes in for another option.

Third Generation Jiu-Jitsu

Rener Gracie, son of Rorion Gracie and grandson of Helio Gracie has made a name of his own despite his popular last name. Having submitted in competition the likes of 2004 BJJ World Champion Cassio Werneck, UFC regular Joe Stevenson and 2 time World Champion Fabio Leopoldo, Rener is already a force in the Jiu Jitsu world even though he is only 24. Running the famed Gracie Academy with his brother Ryron, Rener is an excellent combination of technique and hard work. For more on the gym, Rener and the Gracie family log on to www.gracieacademy.com.

Side Mount Kimura Set Up to Arm Bar

Rener has RJ in side mount. Notice his hips are flat and he is under hooking RJ's far shoulder.

By placing his forearm on RJ's neck Rener forces RJ to defend with his right arm.

Now Rener can flatten RJ's right arm to the mat and starts to slide his left leg over the arm.

Rener brings his left knee up to RJ's head keeping constant pressure.

From here, if it was MMA, Rener can strike to RJ's face with fists or elbows.

Rener reaches for RJ's right arm with his left hand and elevates RJ's elbow. Now Rener can bring his right leg under RJ's arm.

Now Rener can step over RJ's head.

Rener can go for the Kimura here by grabbing RJ's left wrist with his right hand and coming under RJ's arm with his left hand and grabbing his own wrist.

Going for the arm bar, Rener posts his right foot next to RJ's head and begins to rotate his hips to the mat.

Rener brings his hips in tight to control RJ's movement.

Rener then brings his left leg over the body of RJ...

...so he can break RJ's grip and finish the arm bar.

Everyone knows the incredibly effective striking skills of UFC middleweight champion Anderson Silva but people tend to forget his Brazilian jiu-jitsu skills are top notch as well. His opponents are left to pick their poison; either strike it out and risk getting knocked out or take it to the ground and risk getting submitted. The black belt is also very unorthodox with his ground game making him one of the most exciting fighters to watch today.

For more on Anderson "The Spider" Silva, log on to www.spidersilva.com

Modified Arm Bar from Guard

Anderson has his opponent in his guard with his left hand controlling his opponent's left wrist.

Maintaining his grip, Anderson brings his right arm under his opponent's left arm and grips the back of his neck.

Pulling his head down with his right hand, Anderson brings his right leg up on top of his opponent's left shoulder.

Anderson pushes his opponent's left hand up into his neck.

Now Anderson swings his left leg up on top of his opponent's head setting up the arm bar. His opponent can not defend because his left arm is trapped.

Anderson tightens the lock by pulling his left leg in with his right hand . . .

. . . and finishes by gripping his opponent's wrist and extending the arm bar.

SEE PAGE 176 FOR AN EXCLUSIVE MMA WORLDWIDE PACKAGE DEAL!

Figure Four Lock to Arm Bar

Anderson has his opponent in full guard who is posturing up with his hand on Anderson's neck looking to strike.

To prevent getting hit, Anderson controls his opponent's right arm by gripping his bicep with his left hand.

Anderson grips under his opponent's left leg with his right arm so he can rotate slightly counter clockwise. He also changes his left hand grip to his opponent's wrist and places his left foot on his bicep.

Anderson places his right foot under his opponent's chin while still maintaining all of his grips.

Anderson releases his grip with his left hand and grasps his opponent's left wrist pulling him down into him. Simultaneously he figure fours his left leg over his right.

To finish the arm bar Anderson squeezes his legs together and pushes on his opponent's wrist hyper extending his arm.

Modified Side Choke from Guard

Anderson has his opponent in full guard who is looking to control Anderson's arms and strike.

With his left arm, Anderson pulls his opponent's left arm into his chest.

With both hands, Anderson pushes his opponent's arm to the opposite side of his body.

Anderson grips both his hands together trapping his opponent's arm.

Quickly, Anderson releases his grip and brings his leg in between his hold. He then initiates his grip again looking for the choke.

If the choke is unsuccessful he can attack his opponent's left hand and go for an elbow lock.

Kimura from Guard

Anderson has his opponent in full guard.

Anderson posts his left hand on his opponent's elbow elevating it up off his arm.

He then slides his left hand down to his opponent's wrist while bringing his right hand up and over his opponent's arm. Notice Anderson has lifted his shoulders off the mat.

Now Anderson grabs his own left wrist with his right hand.

From here Anderson drives his opponent's head to the mat . . .

. . . and drives his wrist to his head finishing the kimura.

Sweep Counter to Sweep

Anderson is looking for a kimura on his opponent's right arm.

His opponent defends so Anderson posts his left hand out and attempts to sweep.

Anderson lifts his hips up but his opponent drops his weight down and prevents the sweep.

So Anderson takes his momentum the other way, turning his hips into his opponent, driving his opponent's head and shoulders down with his right hand and bringing his right leg off to the side.

Using the momentum, Anderson slides his right leg into his opponent's base while lifting his left leg up in the air while posting up on his right elbow.

This sends his opponent's back to the mat.

Anderson lands in mount . . .

. . . and posts out maintaining his base to not be reswept.

Arm Triangles

Rigan Machado is an 8th degree black belt in Brazilian Jiu-Jitsu earning his rank under Carlos Gracie Jr. From the age of 14 through 21, Professor Machado won the World Championships every year and every belt division. In Brazilian jiu-jitsu he amassed a record of 365 wins and two losses, both losses were against Rickson Gracie.

Rigan Machado is pictured with Marcos Santos of NYBJJ Academy in NYC. Marcos Santos holds a Black Belt 3rd Degree as awarded by the International Brazilian Jiu Jitsu Federation, IBJJF.

Visit: www.nybjj.com
Photography by John Ricard, www.johnricard.com

Arm Triangle from Back

Rigan begins in back mount position.

Rigan fakes a lapel choke while controlling Marcos' right arm. While Marcos is focused on defending the choke, Rigan uses his left leg to control Marcos' hips.

Rigan releases control of Marcos' lapel and uses his own shoulder to press Marcos' arm into Marcos' neck and shoulder. Rigan maintains his hook inside Marcos' left leg.

Keeping control of Marcos' arm, Rigan uses his left leg to assume mount position.

Rigan assumes full mount. Rigan uses his left shoulder to push Marcos' arm across his body.

As Marcos' attention moves to escaping the mount, Rigan dismounts to assume side control. Rigan maintains his arm and shoulder control on Marcos.

Rigan pushes his weight onto Marcos' arm and uses his left arm to apply pressure to Marcos' neck. Rigan also uses his right arm to pressure his own head, to transfer maximum pressure to the choke.

Reverse angle of the choke.

SEE PAGE 176 FOR AN EXCLUSIVE MMA WORLDWIDE PACKAGE DEAL!

Side Choke from Side Mount

Rigan secures an opposite side underhook while keeping Marcos in side control.

Rigan tightens his control on Marcos by using a Gable Grip.

Marcos begins to push against Rigan's neck to reduce the pressure on Marcos' neck. Rigan uses this as an opportunity to set up an arm triangle on Marcos.

Rigan moves his head to the side of Marcos' arm and uses his own head to apply pressure to Marcos' arm and neck. Rigan controls Marcos so he cannot escape Rigan's side control.

Rigan steps over Marcos' hips as if he were trying to assume mount position. He maintains his control of Marcos' arm and neck.

Rigan does assume mount position and instead passes his right knee over Marcos' body to assume opposite side control.

While maintaining opposite side control, Rigan uses his left arm on his own head to increase the pressure on Marcos' neck and shoulder. Rigan's arm position is similar to the one used in a rear naked choke.

Side Choke from Scarf Hold

Rigan begins by passing Marcos' guard into side control.

Rigan secures an opposite side underhook on Marcos' left arm and begins controlling Marcos' right arm at the elbow.

Rigan secures side control.

From side control, Rigan pushes Marcos' arm down in an effort to make Marcos believe that Rigan will apply an armlock.

Marcos defends the arm submission attempt and tries to push Rigan away.

Rigan moves his head to the side of Marcos' arm and pushes his body weight into Marcos' arm and neck.

Using his left arm to lock his arms tightly in place, Rigan secures an arm triangle on Marcos.

Arm Triangles

Arm Triangle from Mount

Rigan attains the mount position.

Rigan grapevines Marcos' legs.

Rigan controls Marcos' head and uses his right shoulder to put pressure on Marcos' head.

Marcos uses his right arm to push against Rigan to relieve the pressure on Marcos' neck.

Rigan passes his head to the side of Marcos' arm.

Jorge brings his hips up for a right hook to the head . . .

Using his head and a Gable Grip underneath Marcos to keep pressure on marcos' arm and neck, Rigan removes himself from mount position.

Rigan assumes a side control and uses his head and shoulder to apply the arm triangle on Marcos.

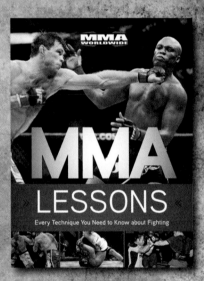